Quick & Easy English Punctuation

Compiled & Edited by
Richard De A'Morelli

SPECTRUM INK PUBLISHING
"Tomorrow's Great Classics Today"

Quick & Easy English Punctuation

Copyright © 2017 by Spectrum Ink Publishing

Published simultaneously in Canada & the United States

First Edition: 11 February 2017

All rights reserved worldwide under U.S., Canadian, and international copyright treaties. No part of this book may be reproduced or transmitted by any means including photocopying, scanning, or digital reproduction. This content may not be posted on any blog, website, or social network without the publisher's knowledge and written consent, except for brief quotations embodied in critical articles and reviews.

The views expressed in this work are solely those of the author and do not necessarily reflect the views of the publisher. The publisher hereby disclaims all such views and statements.

ISBN numbers:
978-1-988236-21-6 ~ mobi
978-1-988236-50-6 ~ paperback

Spectrum Ink Canada
Vancouver, British Columbia

Spectrum Ink USA
San Luis Obispo, California

Online:
http://vu.org/books

What This Book Will Do for You

Punctuation, often misused or dismissed as trivial by many writers, is more important than you might think. It allows your words to tell their story. These small but crucial marks in your sentences are like road signs; without them, readers can get lost in a confusing jumble of words. Learning basic rules of punctuation is a must if you want to write well. Fortunately, the rules are easy to learn, and you will find many helpful shortcuts in these pages.

This book is intended as a desktop reference on English punctuation for writers, college students, ESL learners, and those in the workplace who are called upon to create well-written documents. It offers bite-size tutorials and simple advice on how to use commas, semicolons, and other punctuation marks in all kinds of writing, both fiction and nonfiction. It also will teach you that punctuation rules are not set in stone; rather, you have choices. You'll discover that you can rearrange your sentences and use punctuation creatively to make your writing more interesting.

Quick & Easy English Punctuation is aimed at these readers who may benefit from this useful guide:

> ✓ Writers of all skill levels will learn how to recognize and fix punctuation errors in their manuscripts, and how to use the various marks to add clarity and sparkle to their prose.

> ✓ Students can use these rules to correctly punctuate term papers and other academic writing.

> ✓ Teachers can use this book to help students learn basic concepts of punctuation without the stress and tears.

> ✓ ESL/EFL learners will benefit from the many short, easy-to-understand examples provided in the book.

> ✓ Employees can follow these rules to create well-written reports, manuals, and other documents in the workplace.

Read any chapter of this book, follow the simple punctuation rules, and you will see a fast improvement in the quality of your writing. Read a chapter a day, and in two weeks, you will be sufficiently adept in punctuation that you'll be able to add a touch of style and polish to everything you write.

This book expands on the author's bestselling writing guide, *Elements of Style 2017*. It includes material drawn from that book but delves deeper into the subject of punctuation, providing more examples and an additional eighty pages of content. Once you have mastered the concepts in this book, you may wish to continue on to *Elements of Style 2017,* which offers a comprehensive primer on English grammar, available at http://www.amazon.com/dp/B01MD0396I in Kindle and paperback editions from Amazon.com.

About the Author

Richard De A'Morelli published his first magazine article at age fourteen and signed a multi-book contract with a traditional publisher at eighteen. Since then, he has published fifteen nonfiction books on writing and inspirational topics, three novels under pseudonyms, and 500+ by-lined newspaper and magazine articles.

Beyond freelance writing, Richard has 30+ years of experience as a professional editor. He was a by-lined editorial staff member to the late, bestselling author Irving Wallace, and he has held management-level editorial positions with book and magazine publishers. He has produced and taught a dozen online courses on writing, Web design, and motivational topics at Virtual University. He also has taught journalism, writing, and self-help courses in traditional classroom settings at Los Angeles Valley College and Learning Tree University in Southern California.

Richard currently resides on the scenic Central Coast of California, south of Morro Bay, with his wife and a menagerie of cats, raccoons, and other wildlife. He freelances full-time as a writer, editor and Web developer.

Homepage	http://my.vu.org/writers/richard
Facebook Profile	http://facebook.com/writer2
Author's Page	http://facebook.com/jedi.editor
Twitter	http://twitter.com/jedi_editor
Google+	http://google.com/+RichardDeamorelli

Other Spectrum Ink Books by this Author:

- *Elements of Style 2017*
- *Elements of Style: Classic Edition* (Editor)
- *Live Well. Be Happy.*
- *As a Man Thinks* (Editor)

For details or to order, please visit http://vu.org/books/

Acknowledgments

The content in this book is comprised of original material remixed with updated and revised content drawn from a variety of copyrighted sources used with permission, and public domain materials including: *Practical Grammar and Composition* (Thomas Wood); *English Punctuation* by Benjamin G. Benedict; *A Practical Handbook for Writers and Students* by Paul Allardyce; *NARA Style Guide* (National Archives); *Guide to Marking Written Assignments* (Ian Johnston); *EIA Writing Style Guide* (U.S. Energy Information Administration); and *Government Printing Style Manual* (2008 ed.).

Cover graphic elements licensed from Adobe Stock Photos.

This book makes frequent references to *The Chicago Manual of Style* (16th Edition) and A*P Stylebook* for writers of American English; and to *Oxford Style Guide* for writers of British English. Examples and discussion on stylistic differences are provided throughout the book. This current work is not intended as a substitute for any of these style guides. It may be used as a learning tool and a quick-reference alternative, but editors and publishers should rely on the latest version of their preferred style guide as the final authority.

Contents

1: WHY PUNCTUATION MATTERS 9
2: THE FULL STOP (PERIOD) 17
3: THE COMMA 27
4: THE SEMICOLON 55
5: THE COLON 63
6: THE QUESTION MARK 71
7: THE EXCLAMATION POINT 77
8: DASHES AND HYPHENS 83
9: THE ELLIPSIS 101
10: PARENTHESES & BRACKETS 107
11: QUOTATION MARKS 115
12: APOSTROPHES 129
13: OTHER SYMBOLS 139
CONCLUSION 151
GLOSSARY 153
More Books from Spectrum Ink 158

Chapter 1

Why Punctuation Matters

> "The night is falling down around us. Meteors rain like fireworks, quick rips in the seam of the dark... Every second, another streak of silver glows: parentheses, exclamation points, commas — a whole grammar made of light."
>
> Jodi Picoult
> "My Sister's Keeper"

Many writers assume that grammar is boring and punctuation is trivial. In reality, grammar is the mortar that holds your words together in a coherent fashion, and punctuation is the finishing touch that makes good writing great and written language more effective by allowing words to tell their story. The lowly commas, periods, and other marks inserted into your sentences are like road signs; without them, readers would get lost in a confusing jumble of words. Punctuation directs the reader's eye from word to word, from one sentence to the next, indicating thoughtful pauses by commas, graceful transitions to new thoughts by periods, interrupted action by dashes and ellipses, queries raised by question marks, anger and surprise by exclamation points, and more. By using these marks artfully, you provide a window into your thoughts and the inner sanctuary of your mind where the winds of creativity blow; where you hear the whispered pauses and stops in your narratives and dialogue, represented by the punctuation marks that you write into your sentences.

Author and literary agent Noah Lukeman observes in *A Dash of Style*: "There is an underlying rhythm to all text. Sentences crashing fall like the waves of the sea, and work unconsciously on the reader. Punctuation is the music of language. As a conductor can influence the experience of the song by manipulating its rhythm, so can punctuation influence the reading experience, bringing out the best (or worst) in a text."

Without punctuation, everything we write would be susceptible to ambiguity and misinterpretation. Even when punctuation is used, but it is used incorrectly, readers are at risk of serious misunderstandings. You might think short sentences would have clear meanings, but just a few words can be perplexing if punctuated incorrectly. Consider this example, where the meaning is quite different, depending on whether two commas are used or omitted:

> The prisoner said the witness was a despicable thief.

> The prisoner, said the witness, was a despicable thief.

Many hilarious examples of short sentences with flawed or missing punctuation have been featured in memes shared on social networks. Here's another:

> Let's eat Grandma! I'm starving!

Poor Grandma. For lack of a comma, she is at risk of becoming someone's dinner. When we insert the missing comma, grandma's fate is brighter.

> Let's eat, Grandma! I'm starving!

Punctuation as it is used today is a relatively recent innovation. The invention of the printing press made it necessary to have a well-defined system for using the various marks that had existed for centuries. Previously, the personal preferences of scribes had determined how these marks were written. With the dawn of an era in which books could be reproduced faster and more easily than by hand copying came the need for a systematic approach to recording and sharing the written word. A widely understood system of punctuating those writings to enhance clarity was also a necessity.

Early writings dating back to the dawn of the Latin alphabet, which was introduced by the Etruscans in the eighth century BCE, contained strings of letters with no spacing between words or sentences, and no punctuation marks of any kind. The first such mark to be used was the dot, or period. Its purpose was to provide a resting place for the eye and to help a little in grouping the letters into clauses and sentences. It was used at the end of a sentence, to indicate abbreviations, and as an aesthetic ornament between the letters of an inscription.

Later, during the manuscript period, a variety of marks and systems of pointing came into use. For a considerable time, the location of the dot indicated its force. Placed high, it had the force of a period. Placed in a middle position (·) it had the force of a comma. Placed low (.) it had the force of a semicolon.

The invention of the printing press by Johannes Gutenberg (c. 1398-1468), a German blacksmith, heralded new requirements. The early printers were scholars too, and for years, their main concern was the sharing of ancient writings with the world, so they had to be the students, critics, and editors of the old manuscripts they printed. They borrowed most of their punctuation from Greek grammarians, but sometimes adapted the meanings. The semicolon, for instance, is the Greek mark of interrogation, or question mark.

The punctuation marks now in use, and that we will discuss in this present book are:

1. **Full stop:** marks the end of a sentence
2. **Comma:** separates clauses and phrases
3. **Semicolon:** separates different statements
4. **Colon:** the transition point of the sentence
5. **Question mark:** asks a question for an answer
6. **Exclamation point:** expresses surprise, shock, or anger
7. **Dash:** marks abruptness or irregularity, indicates range
8. **Hyphen:** breaks words; also forms compound words

9. **Ellipsis:** indicates omission from a quoted passage
10. **Parentheses:** enclose interpolations in the sentence
11. **Brackets:** enclose irregularities in the sentence
12. **Quotation mark:** sets off quoted words and passages
13. **Apostrophe:** marks elisions and the possessive case
14. **Other symbols** widely used in contemporary writing

Two systems of punctuation are used in the English language: the *open system*, sometimes called the *easy system*, and the *close system*. The open system omits points wherever possible, and it is used in common forms of composition. The closed system uses points wherever possible and when such points are of importance in precise composition of every sort, such as contracts and legal documents. The tendency today, sometimes pushed too far, is toward an extremely open style of punctuation. The general attitude of writers is that you must justify the use of a punctuation mark rather justify its omission.

The chapters in this book provide a detailed overview of the functions of punctuation marks and everyday rules for their use. These rules are flexible, though, and they are useless if not applied intelligently. No set of rules could ever be devised that would work in every situation or relieve the writer, editor, or proofreader from the necessity of thinking. Writing and editing cannot be reduced to an exact science, and the same applies to proofreading and the use of punctuation.

In addition to the rules of grammar and punctuation, so-called style rules help writers aim for consistency and high quality in their prose. These rules clarify a wide range of issues, from rules on capitalization and punctuation, to hyphenating compound nouns and questions on whether to use commas, parentheses, or dashes to set off a particular clause. Style rules fill in the gray areas that exist because grammar rules tend to be broad.

The goal of style is to enforce consistency—a must for writers who wish to make a favorable impression on readers and express written ideas in the clearest manner possible. For instance, every major style guide includes a rule that advises how numbers should be written. The most widely used handbook, *The Chicago Manual of Style*, recommends that numbers up to one hundred inclusive should be spelled out, and numbers over one hundred should be written as digits. So, we would write: *The alphabet has twenty-six letters, and a year has 365 days.*

When we stray from consistent adherence to style rules, we may end up with a haphazard jumble of digits and spelled-out numbers as in the following passage:

> ✘ Nine men stood by the wall, and 4 women stood next to the 2 cars. When the police approached the 9 men, they scattered, and the four women jumped into the two cars and sped away.

The lack of consistency in the way that the numbers are handled in the above sentence detracts from the clarity and overall quality of the writing and should always be avoided. Let's rewrite the sentence using Chicago Style, spelling out the numbers, and we will eliminate the unnecessary repetition of those numbers in the second sentence. The result flows considerably better:

> ☺ Nine men stood by the wall, and four women stood next to the two cars. When the police approached the men, they scattered, and the women jumped into the cars and sped away.

Some novice writers believe that following style rules is unnecessary, and diligent self-editing and proofreading aren't important—after all, it's the story that counts, right? But that's not the case. Reader surveys confirm that today's book buyers expect published material to be well-written and edited, with few or no typos. Self-published books thrown up on Amazon.com with little attention given to editing typically sell poorly and receive negative reviews from readers.

Numerous writing style guides exist today. The most popular include *The Chicago Manual of Style*, the bible of editors in fiction genres and relied upon by some nonfiction publishers too; *AP Stylebook*, used by most journalists who write for news publications and websites; APA format, developed by the American Psychological Association and used in education, psychology, and social science writing; *MLA Style*, an academic style used in the humanities and English studies. In the United Kingdom, the principal authority on style is *The Oxford Style Guide*. Other lesser known style guides are used today in government, academia, science, and in the publishing industry.

Style guides are filled with rules on grammar and punctuation. A professional editor may spend months learning the nuances of these rules. This presents a high bar for writers who want to submit a manuscript to a publisher with the imprimatur of being cleanly edited and proofread, and for those who wish to self-publish but cannot afford the expense of an editor or proofreader. Adding confusion to mix, some of the advice given by the leading style guides is contradictory. For instance, Chicago Style requires the use of the serial or Oxford comma, while AP Style advises against it. So, if you are editing to AP Style and use a serial comma, it's an error; if you are following Chicago Style and don't use a serial comma, that's an error. Some writers today don't even know what a serial comma is! For the sake of clarity, it is a comma placed before the coordinating conjunction in a list of three or more items. The first sentence below has a serial comma after *pencils*; it is omitted in the second sentence.

> **Chicago Style:**
> She bought pens, pencils, and paper.
>
> **AP Style:**
> She bought pens, pencils and paper.

Similarly, Chicago Style and AP Style both require that the period at the end of a dialogue passage be placed inside the closing quotation mark. But Oxford Style advises that the period should be placed outside the closing quote mark as shown below:

> **Chicago and AP Style:**
> Mary said, "Some of these rules are confusing."
>
> **Oxford Style:**

Mary said, "Some of these rules are confusing".

Ultimately, whichever style manual you follow, study the guidelines and then diligently adhere to them to achieve consistency throughout the creative process of writing, editing, and proofreading. Unlike grammar, which gives us a set of rules that generally should not be broken, style rules are more flexible and, to some extent, reflect the preferences of individual publishers (house rules). These guidelines help us decide when to spell numbers, whether to use serial commas, which words should be capitalized or hyphenated, and address many other small but essential questions.

At the same time, it's important to recognize that style guides may differ, and no two editors will ever produce the same result, even if they both follow the same rules, because editing, like writing, is a creative process that involves some degree of subjectivity. Even so, adhering to style rules will enhance readability and give your work the finished quality and polish your readers will likely expect and will certainly appreciate.

Good writing is built on patterns, so whether you are writing a news story, a press release, a science fiction novel, or a sizzling love story, develop a consistent writing style and stay with it. Don't refer to an iPhone in one paragraph, a cell phone in the next paragraph, and a mobile device on the following page. Switching back and forth does not add interest to your prose; it merely confuses readers and makes it more difficult for them to follow what you are saying.

These next chapters will introduce you to the basic rules of English punctuation and capitalization. If you apply them consistently, your writing quality will quickly improve. On that note, let's begin this learning adventure!

Chapter 2

The Full Stop (Period)

> "Punctuation marks are the traffic signals of language: they tell us to slow down, notice this, take a detour, and stop."
>
> Lynne Truss
> "Eats, Shoots & Leaves"

The full stop, or period, is the simplest punctuation mark in the English language. It marks the end of a statement or command that forms a complete sentence. Of Greek origin, it came into use around 300 BCE. The term *period* became popular in the eighteenth century when printers began using it to refer to a full point—a dot on the baseline of printed matter. By the 1800s, it was synonymous with *full stop* in British English. Today, the term is used more commonly in American English. Besides terminating a declaratory sentence, the period has a number of other uses as described below.

2.01 | Every full sentence that is not an **interrogatory** (a question), **exclamatory** (expresses surprise, anger, or shock), or an interrupted thought (see Rule 2.07), must be terminated with a full stop.

2.02 | Sentences and main clauses should not be run together without a clear and appropriate break between the end of one main independent idea and the start of the next one. This error creates a **run-on sentence**, or **fused sentence**, a basic punctuation error that can cause ambiguity and confusion for readers.

The first example below is a run-on sentence because it lacks a clear break between the two main ideas. The reader cannot tell where exactly the first idea ends and the second idea begins. In the second sentence, a full stop is placed at the end of the first complete idea.

> ✘ We arrived at the crime scene first an hour later, the police drove up.

> ☺ We arrived at the scene first. An hour later, the police drove up.

2.03 | Use a full stop after a single word that stands as a sentence; for example, a short reply to an interrogatory, such as *Yes*, *No*, and *Maybe*.

> "Yes. I ate the ice cream."

2.04 | As a general rule, do not insert a period until the sentence is grammatically complete. But some parts of the sentence may be implied or left for the reader to fill in.

> Roman emperor Marcus Aurelius observed: "Very little is needed to make a happy life; it is all within yourself, in your way of thinking." Great thinker. Great saying.

The phrases *Great thinker* and *Great saying* are not complete sentences but are treated as such and terminated with a full stop because each phrase implies a complete idea that the reader will grasp. Sentence fragments such as these should be avoided in formal and technical writing, but they are used in fiction and casual forms of writing.

2.05 | Use a period after an indirect question (a question meant as a suggestion or declaratory statement where no answer is expected). When the indirect question is exclamatory, as in the fourth sentence reflecting indignation, an exclamation point may be used instead.

> What did you expect me to say.
>
> Will you shut up.
>
> May we have your attention.
>
> Just who do you think you are!

2.06 | Do not use a period after a quotation mark that is preceded by another terminating mark, such as a period or a question mark.

✗ Mary said: "Hurry up or we will leave without you.".

☺ Mary said: "Hurry up or we will leave without you."

✗ The teacher asked, "What is your problem?".

☺ The teacher asked, "What is your problem?"

✗ Jim frowned and mumbled, "But I thought...".

☺ Jim frowned and mumbled, "But I thought..."

2.07 | When a sentence is deliberately interrupted or left unfinished, a dash or ellipsis may be used in place of a full stop. Generally, use a dash to indicate abrupt interruption, and an ellipsis to indicate that the sentence trails off.

Sentence ends abruptly; use a dash:
The doorbell rang, and when Jill opened the front door, she shouted, "No! How can you be—"

Sentence trails off; use an ellipsis:
The doorbell rang, and when Jill opened the front door, she whispered, "Oh, it's you..."

2.08 | Do not place a period at the end of a sentence if the last word in the sentence is an abbreviation that also ends with a period.

✗ The product was manufactured by Alcoa Inc..

☺ The product was manufactured by Alcoa Inc.

2.09 | Use a single space after the full stop between sentences. Double spacing after sentences was common back in the day of typewriters, but today, this practice is considered by most to be old-fashioned and should be avoided.

2.10 | When writing time expressions, use a colon to separate the hours and minutes, and follow the numbers with *a.m.* or *p.m.* Some style guides indicate that *A.M.* and *P.M.* are acceptable, or the periods may be omitted from the upper case letters, as in *8:30 AM.* Do not use lower case letters without periods, since *am* is a distinct word and its use in time expressions may confuse readers. Leave a space between the numbers and the abbreviation.

> ✗ **Avoid:** 5:30 am (lower case, no periods)
>
> ☺ **Preferred:** 4:30 p.m., 9:00 a.m., 7 p.m.
>
> ☺ **Acceptable:** 4:30 P.M., 4:30 PM (in some style guides)

2.11 | In academic, technical, and other formal writing, avoid using the expressions *o'clock, in the morning, in the afternoon, in the evening,* or *at night* when writing times. These expressions should be limited to character dialogue and narratives in fiction writing.

> ✗ five in the morning; nine at night; four o'clock, twelve midnight (avoid in formal writing)
>
> ☺ 5:00 a.m., 9 p.m., 12:00 a.m.
>
> ☺ *Noon* and *midnight* are acceptable in some style guides.

2.12 | When using the twenty-four-hour clock, write the time as a four-digit number followed by a space and the abbreviation *hr.* For instance, *3:30 p.m.* would be expressed as *1530 hr.* This practice is not common except in certain applications, such as air travel timetables and military time.

2.13 | Whatever method you use to write times, consistently follow the same style throughout your manuscript so that all your references to times are expressed in the same manner. Avoid writing *5:30 a.m.,* and a few pages later, *7 PM.* Such variations, although trivial, will distract readers, and some may wonder why you are switching from one format to another.

2.14 | The correct way to write the abbreviated form of *United States* depends on your style guide, and can even depend on how you use the term. The preference in Chicago Style has changed from *U.S.* to *US* with no periods; but AP Style requires U.S.—unless it is in a headline, and then it's US.

> **Chicago Style:** Americans elect a new president every four years.

> **AP Style:** Americans elect a new president every four years.
> but **AP Style headline:** US Inflation Rate Spikes in January

2.15 | The period is used in some abbreviations, but style guides vary. Chicago Style minimizes the use of periods in abbreviations, while AP Style calls for more frequent use, as the following examples illustrate. For rules on using periods with particular abbreviations, refer to the style guide that you are following for your current project.

Chicago	**AP Style**
PhD	Ph.D.
MA	M.A.
BA	B.A.
JD	J.D.
USSR	U.S.S.R.
US	U.S.
UN	U.N.

2.16 | The abbreviations *i.e.* and *e.g.* derive from Latin terms: i.e., short for *id est,* means "that is"; and e.g., short for *exempli gratia,* means "for example." Both require two periods, as in the preceding sentence, and must be followed by a comma. The terms are generally regarded as unnecessarily formal or stuffy in present-day writing, and it's best to avoid using them; instead, recast the sentence.

> ☺ that is, (or specifically,) California, Oregon, and Washington

> ☺ namely, California, Oregon, and Washington

> ✗ **Correct, but avoid:** i.e., California, Oregon, and Washington

> ☺ for example, apples and pears

☺ including (or such as) apples and pears
✗ **Correct, but avoid:** e.g., apples and pears

2.17 | A period may be used to show the omission of one or more letters in an abbreviated word.

Geo. Jones, Dr. Robt. Smith, John Welch Jr.

2.18 | Special rules apply to periods (and other marks) used with **parentheses**, depending on the placement of the mark. If the content enclosed within parentheses is a phrase (not a complete sentence), write the period *outside* the closing paren. If the content is a complete sentence, write the period *inside* the closing paren. If the content is a sentence and ends with a period, and if the closing paren completes a compound sentence, use a second period outside the closing paren, or rewrite the sentence to avoid this construction.

Phrase enclosed in parentheses:
President Trump continued to use Twitter (as many people had expected).

Full sentence in parentheses, inserted mid-sentence:
NSA document leaker Edward Snowden has been living in Russia (Has anyone seen him alive lately?), and if he was hoping for a pardon from outgoing Pres. Barack Obama, it didn't happen.

Full sentence in parenthesis, at end of sentence:
The alien invasion began on March 13 (UFO skeptics became believers when a laser evaporated New York City instantly.).

2.19 | If a sentence contains more than one **parenthetical reference**, the one at the end is placed before the period, unless an exception applies under Rule 2.18.

Sandstone (see fig. 6) is in every county of Ohio (see fig. 1).

2.20 | Use a period at the end of notes and footnotes. Do not use a period at the end of sources.

☺ **Footnote (use a period):**
Note: GMO is an abbreviation for genetically modified organism.

☺ **Source citation (no period):**
the U.S. Food and Drug Administration

2.21 | In computer terminology, the period is often called a "dot," and it is used in a number of ways: in website addresses, file names, and IP addresses, among others.

> Facebook.com
>
> document.txt
>
> webpage.html
>
> 192.168.0.1

2.22 | Do not use a period after single letters of the alphabet that represent names without specific designation.

> Officer B, Subject A, Brand X, etc.
>
> A said to B that all is well.
>
> Mr. A told Mr. B that the case was closed.
>
> Mr. X (for unknown or censored name)
>
> but Mr. A. does not want to go
> [In this sentence, Mr. A. specifically refers to Mr. Andrews]

2.23 | A period may be used in place of a closing parenthesis after a letter or number that identifies an element in a list or series.

> a. California
> b. Oregon
> c. Washington
>
> 1. apples
> 2. oranges
> 3. lemons

2.24 | Use a period followed by a space after the middle initial in a person's name.

>Daniel D. Tompkins, Ross T. McIntire

2.25 | Do not use a period after Roman numerals written as ordinals.

>King George V
>
>Super Bowl XLII
>
>Apollo XII

2.26 | Use a period after a legend (such as *Figure 1*) when followed by descriptive language beneath a photo, diagram, or other illustration.

>Figure 1. Image of Yellowstone Park
>
>Figure 2. Bart and Betty on vacation in Wyoming

If a legend stands alone with no descriptive language, omit the period.

>Figure 1
>
>Table 2

2.27 | Use a period to separate whole numbers from decimals in a single expression.

>0.15 miles
>
>$5.00
>
>3.65 meters
>
>1.5 ounces

2.28 | A period is sometimes used in place of a comma to indicate thousands in continental European languages.

>3.1415
>
>20.650.537

2.29 | When writing complex or sophisticated sentences and paragraphs for nearly any kind of composition, a writer may at times struggle with where to insert full stops, and whether other punctuation marks would be more appropriate. The degree of the closeness of the thought usually determines whether the sentence should be considered as complete and be terminated by a period, or whether other pauses should be employed.

Consider the following excerpt from a letter written by American patriot John Adams in 1776. For this example, all ending punctuation marks have been removed from the passage.

> **Without full stops:**
>
> The day is past the second day of July, 1776, will be the most memorable epoch in the history of America I am apt to believe that it will be celebrated by succeeding generations as the great anniversary festival it ought to be commemorated as the day of deliverance by solemn acts of devotion to God Almighty it ought to be solemnized by pomp and parade, with shows, games, sports, guns, bells, bonfires, and illumined from one end of the continent to the other from this time forevermore I am well aware of the toil and blood and treasure which it will cost us to maintain this declaration and defend these states—*Letter of John Adams, July 3d, 1776*

To punctuate this passage according to the directions in this chapter, we place the first period after *past*. *The day is past* has its own subject and finite verb, is not joined to the subsequent words by any connective such as *and, but,* or *because,* or by a relative pronoun, and is not closely allied to these subsequent words in meaning. Thus, we have a complete sentence. For the same reasons, we insert a period after *America, festival, Almighty, forevermore, and states.*

> ☺ **Correctly punctuated:**
>
> The day is past. The second day of July, 1776, will be the most memorable epoch in the history of America. I am apt to believe that it will be celebrated by succeeding generations as the great anniversary festival. It ought to be commemorated as the day of deliverance by solemn acts of devotion to God

> Almighty. It ought to be solemnized by pomp and parade, with shows, games, sports, guns, bells, bonfires, and illumined from one end of the continent to the other from this time forevermore. I am well aware of the toil and blood and treasure which it will cost us to maintain this declaration and defend these states. —*Letter of John Adams, July 3, 1776.*

2.30 | In writing projects where the writer strives for well-developed and correctly punctuated prose, novice writers, students, and ESL learners may have difficulty in determining what is or is not a complete sentence. Study, care, and practice will remove that difficulty to a great extent. As we saw in the preceding example, a sentence is generally complete and should terminate with a period when it has a separate subject and verb from the sentence that follows, and is not joined to it by a **connective conjunction** such as *and, but, for, or as,* and when in meaning and construction it is not dependent upon it, and is not closely allied to it.

In the following sentence, the use of *and* in the second clause, and the intimate connection of the thought with that of the first, show that the sense is not complete, and it should not be followed by the period.

> I believe the young man is honest, and I shall never change my opinion until the contrary is proved.

If the *and* is omitted, the two parts then may be viewed and punctuated as two complete sentences, as:

> I believe the young man to be honest. I shall never change my opinion until the contrary is proved.

Chapter 3

The Comma

> *"I was working on the proof of one of my poems all the morning, and took out a comma. In the afternoon I put it back again."*
>
> — Oscar Wilde

Commas cause much confusion among writers. Browse through any book on Amazon or another online bookstore, and you will likely find stray or missing commas in the first few pages, even in professionally edited books. Incorrectly placed or missing commas might seem trivial, but these errors can make a book or report seem unpolished, and they can be annoying to readers who notice them.

If you want to improve the quality of your writing, invest a few hours in reading this chapter and memorizing a set of simple rules. What you will learn should help you to conquer comma chaos in your prose. Your readers will thank you, fellow writers will be impressed that you took the time to polish your work, and you will have a book or other document that you can be proud to publish or share with others.

The rules for using commas have changed over the years, and punctuation rules will continue to change as the English language evolves. Certain rules pertaining to commas are etched in stone; in other cases, comma usage is subjective, and the rules are applied in different ways from one writer or editor to the next.

What you need to remember, first and foremost, is this simple principle: a comma indicates a pause. As you read through a piece of writing, when you reach a comma, it's a signal that you should pause briefly before reading the next word. As a rule of thumb, you can figure out whether a comma is needed in a particular place by reading your paragraph and noticing where the natural pauses occur. If you come to a point where you feel a natural urge to pause for a second, chances are a comma should be placed there.

Consider this sentence published in a popular consumer magazine:

> Rachel Ray finds inspiration in cooking her family and her dog.

This construction is flawed and creates confusion for the reader. We can be fairly certain that Rachel Ray does not enjoy cooking either her family or her dog. Read the sentence again, but this time, look for the natural pauses, and that is where commas should have been added. Let's rewrite the sentence and add those commas:

> Rachel Ray finds inspiration in cooking, her family, and her dog.

Now this statement makes sense and conveys the message as the writer no doubt intended.

Read through your own manuscript and apply the same principle—look for natural pauses. Do you have missing commas? If so, add them. Conversely, if you find a comma where you don't feel a natural pause occurs, consider removing it.

Remember: the comma should help to clarify the meaning of your words in a sentence and prevent ambiguity by showing the separation and relationship of those words to one another. If your readers might find a sentence confusing without a comma, put one in. If your words are clear enough without a comma, you can often omit it. This is a good rule to follow when in doubt.

Let's review some basic punctuation rules that should help you to eliminate comma chaos from your writing.

Comma Rules Simplified

3.01 | Use a comma when two complete sentences (also called independent clauses) are separated by a **conjunction** (*and, but, or,* and so on). When we apply this rule to the following examples, all three would require a comma at the end of the first complete sentence, and before the connecting conjunction.

> [Complete sentence], but [complete sentence].
>
> [Complete sentence], or [complete sentence].
>
> [Complete sentence], and [complete sentence].

When writing two complete sentences, you have the option of combining them into a compound sentence by using a comma followed by a conjunction, or writing them as two sentences with a period after each. Is one better than the other? It depends on a number of things; the length of the two sentences, the grammatical structure of each, and the flow of nearby sentences. To decide, read the full paragraph, first with the two clauses connected by a conjunction, and then as two distinct sentences. Whichever flows better is usually the right choice.

> ☺ I want to make dinner, but I can't get the stove to work.
>
> ☺ John bought groceries, Jill picked up her prescription, and Mary fiddled with her phone.
>
> ☺ I was hungry, so I went to the store.

These next examples are complete sentences. Although each has a conjunction (the word *and*) that connects one part of the sentence to another, the phrase that follows the conjunction is not a full sentence; thus, no comma.

> ✗ Paul pumped the gas, and got a soda.
>
> ☺ Paul pumped the gas and got a soda.
>
> ✗ I was hungry, and went for dinner.
>
> ☺ I was hungry and went for dinner.

3.02 | Use commas to separate three or more items in a list. Don't forget the comma between the last two items; this comma is called a **serial comma** (or an Oxford comma), and it is required by a majority of style guides (Chicago Style, APA Style, MLA Style, US Government Printing Office; and in the United Kingdom, Oxford Style). But AP Style and the Canadian Press stylebook advise against its use; so if your current writing project requires that you follow either of these style guides, do not use serial commas.

In the following examples, a serial comma is required after *oranges* and after *peaches* in the first sentence; and a serial comma after *white* in the second.

> ✗ Mary likes apples, oranges and plums; Betty prefers lemons, peaches and apricots.
>
> ☺ Mary likes apples, oranges, and plums; Betty prefers lemons, peaches, and apricots.
>
> ✗ The American flag is red, white and blue.
>
> ☺ The American flag is red, white, and blue.

Sometimes the serial comma is required for clarity, even if your style guide advises against its use. Placing a comma after *Christine* in the sentence below adds two people to the meaning and eliminates an obvious absurdity that needs to be rewritten.

> ✗ Two boys, Christine and Michelle, went home.
> [two people]
>
> ☺ Two boys, Christine, and Michelle went home.
> [four people]

3.03 | Use the comma to separate the parts of a compound sentence when those parts are short and closely connected in their thought.

> John carried the suitcase, I the hat box, and William the umbrella.

3.04 | If the last item in the list has more than one part, write the comma before the first conjunction. In this next example, the serial comma goes after *socks*, not after *laptop*.

☺ For my trip I packed shirts, pants, socks, and my laptop and phone.

Here's another good example of why you should use a serial comma.

✗ After being confirmed as UN ambassador, Nikki Haley thanked her parents, Donald Trump and Paul Ryan.

Without the serial comma, the sentence implies that Haley's parents are Donald Trump and Paul Ryan, an absurdity. Adding a comma after *Trump* remedies this problem.

☺ After being confirmed as UN ambassador, Nikki Haley thanked her parents, Donald Trump, and Paul Ryan.

3.05 | Do not use a serial comma when all the elements in the sentence are separated by conjunctions.

✗ He talked, and smoked, and read.

✗ He talked and smoked, and read.

☺ He talked and smoked and read.

☺ He talked, smoked, and read.

3.06 | Do not use a comma in a **compound predicate** (a sentence that has one subject and two verbs).

✗ The documents are now on display, and may be viewed by the public.

☺ The documents are now on display and may be viewed by the public.

✗ Lewis and Clark endured many hardships, but finally prevailed.

☺ Lewis and Clark endured many hardships but finally prevailed.

3.07 | Writing a comma after a short introductory phrase of fewer than four words is optional in most cases and left to the writer's discretion. But if the meaning of the sentence would be unclear or the construction awkward without the comma, use it.

> **Comma optional:**
>
> In addition, federal taxes are added to the price of gasoline.
>
> In 2016, Congress passed a continuing budget resolution.
>
> **Comma required for clarity:**
>
> ✗ In April 2016 1,406 documents were released.
>
> ☺ In April 2016, 1,406 documents were released.

3.08 | An introductory phrase of four words or longer should be followed by a comma to make the sentence easier to read.

> When Navy destroyers engaged North Vietnamese torpedo boats in 1964, the United States officially entered the Vietnam War.

Sometimes it is better to avoid writing a long introductory phrase and instead change the order of the components in the sentence so that no comma is needed. Whether this is practical depends on what you want to emphasize in the sentence.

> The United States officially entered the Vietnam War when Navy destroyers engaged North Vietnamese torpedo boats in battle in 1964.

3.09 | In a sentence where a comma would not ordinarily be used before a conjunction, and the conjunction is omitted, use a comma.

> I pay this tribute to the memory of that noble, reverend, learned, excellent person.

3.10 | Where a comma would be used if a conjunction were present, a stronger point, such as the semicolon, may be used if the conjunction is omitted.

Compound sentence, comma before the conjunction:

We must be strong and stand tall. The cause of freedom demands it, and our dignity as human beings requires it.

Conjunction omitted, semicolon inserted:

We must be strong and stand tall. The cause of freedom demands it; our dignity as human beings requires it.

3.11 | Use a comma to set off a **participial phrase**. A participial phrase begins with a **present participle** (a word formed from a verb and ending in -*ing*), or a **past participle** (a similar word but ending in -*ed*).

> Apologizing for the scandal, the candidate dropped out of the race.
>
> Gifted with this talent, her books were sure to be bestsellers.
>
> Having divided the estate, the family members returned to cordial relations.
>
> Angered by a critical reporter, the president fired off a series of early-morning tweets.

3.12 | Words used in direct address must be set off from the rest of the sentence by a comma. But if such words are expressed in an exclamatory manner, reflecting shock, anger, or the like, an exclamation point may be used instead of the comma after the word of address.

> "You, sir, are the one to whom I refer."
>
> "James, come here."
>
> "Citizens of Rome, hear my plan."
>
> "Father! You should be ashamed of yourself!"

3.13 | Do not use a comma after an introductory phrase followed by a verb.

> ✗ Remembering the past, makes the woman unhappy.
>
> ☺ Remembering the past makes the woman unhappy.

3.14 | Use a comma to separate two adjectives that modify the same noun; but if one modifies both the other adjective and the noun, no comma is required.

> an honest, upright man
>
> an old, broken toy
>
> She wore a stained blue dress.

3.15 | When two words are combined into a single idea and modified by a single adjective, do not use a comma. But if more than one modifying adjective is present, use a comma on those preceding adjectives.

> An old black coat
>
> A bright blue sky

In the two sentences above, *black coat* and *blue sky* refer to single concepts. Both sentences have only one modifying adjective (*old* refers to the black coat, and *bright* to the blue sky); hence, neither requires a comma. But in the two sentences below, *tattered* and *dazzling* are additional modifiers and require commas.

> A tattered, old black coat
>
> A dazzling, bright blue sky

3.16 | **Coordinate adjectives** (adjectives that can be used in any order without changing the meaning of the sentence), require a comma between each adjective. If the order of the adjectives is not interchangeable, then omit the commas.

> He was a bearded, old, dirty, poor, starving man.
> [Adjectives are interchangeable; thus, use commas.]
>
> She was an impoverished American college student.
> [Adjectives cannot be changed around, so no commas.]

Also, Rule 3.15 applies: not all adjectives are modifying and, thus, don't require commas. In the next two examples, *swift streams* and *cheap motherboards* are not single ideas; *swift* refers to the speed of the water, and *cheap* refers to the price of the motherboards. But a *tributary stream* is a certain type of stream, *short* is the only modifier, therefore, no comma. Similarly, a *desktop computer* is a certain kind of computer, and *fast* is the only modifier, so no comma.

>short, swift streams; but short tributary streams

>fast, cheap motherboards; and fast desktop computers

3.17 | Phrases or clauses in **apposition** (meaning they further identify or describe a noun or pronoun immediately in front of them) are nonrestrictive. Set them off with commas at the start and finish.

>Prof. Bonnie Jones, a professor at St. Mary's College, introduced the guest speaker, Dr. Wendy Simon, director of the County Health Department.

3.18 | Omit the comma when an appositive is a single phrase or a compound name.

>The poet Longfellow was born in Portland.

>Democrat Alice Baily of Wisconsin.

>Joe's brother Gerald was appointed. *(Joe has several brothers)*

>The hijacker Jack Smith was shot dead.

3.19 | **Parenthetical expressions** (also called nonrestrictive or nonessential phrases) require punctuation. Usually, they are set off from the rest of the sentence by commas. Parenthetical expressions may consist of a single word, a phrase, a clause, or a dependent sentence, as the following:

><u>Truly</u>, this was news to me.

>He spoke, <u>as his fans had expected</u>, with charm and conviction.

>These claims are, <u>without a doubt</u>, ridiculous and untrue.

>The captain, <u>who had a reputation for procrastinating</u>, once again could not decide whether to attack or retreat.

>The defendant, <u>whatever excuse he gives for his behavior</u>, is a sadistic killer and should be locked up for life.

A word or expression is parenthetical when the main thought of the sentence would not be affected by its omission. The word *parenthetical* means to place by the side of, and not to include with, another. So, to decide whether an expression is parenthetical or not, omit it and see if the meaning of the sentence is substantially the same. If so, set off the expression by commas, except where exceptions apply, as discussed in Rule 3.20.

> Thomas Jefferson, who wrote the Declaration of Independence, was the third president of the United States.

Here the relative clause, *who wrote the Declaration of Independence*, could be omitted, and the main thought of the sentence remains intact.

3.20 | Single words used parenthetically, and short phrases consisting of just a few words, are not separated from the rest of the sentence by commas when the connection of the thought is close and commas would interfere with the flow of the sentence.

✗ He, too, was included in the proclamation.
☺ He too was included in the proclamation.

✗ She is, in truth, a prodigy.
☺ She is in truth a prodigy.

✗ He will call upon you, if you request it.
☺ He will call upon you if you request it.

✗ He will suffer, unless he changes his behavior.
☺ He will suffer unless he changes his behavior.

When a parenthetical expression does disrupt the flow of the idea, it is nonrestrictive and must be set off by commas. This generally applies to expressions like *in my opinion, according to many sources, by contrast,* and *on the other hand.*

Similarly, **conjunctive adverbs** (*however, moreover, nevertheless, therefore, thus, consequently,* and so on) must be followed by a comma when they start a clause. When they come in the middle of a clause, they should usually be set off by commas.

> The detective's conduct, on the other hand, raises many questions.
>
> This so-called art masterpiece, in my opinion, is a forgery.
>
> Thus, Alexander died while still young; moreover, he left his great dream unfinished.
>
> It is true, as Smith remarked, that the case is strange; it is not, however, unprecedented.

But this latter rule is applied more liberally in contemporary writing, and it is increasingly common to see certain conjunctive adverbs, especially the words *therefore* and *indeed*, written mid-sentence without commas, as long they do not disrupt the flow of the idea.

> ☺ They have, therefore, no cause to be dissatisfied.
>
> ☺ They have therefore no cause to be dissatisfied.
>
> ☺ She was, indeed, surprised that she won the lottery.
>
> ☺ She was indeed surprised that she won the lottery.

3.21 | Slightly parenthetical remarks thrown into a sentence, and where the break is very pronounced, should be set off with commas or other punctuation, such as dashes or parentheses. In the following examples, the parenthetical remarks are underlined and set off by commas. Notice that these remarks can be removed and the sentences remain complete.

> That, <u>if you will let me explain</u>, cannot be done without a permit from the city.
>
> Two men, <u>Chase and Arnold</u>, were injured.
>
> This, <u>I think</u>, is the right course to follow.

3.22 | A **nonrestrictive modifier** is a phrase or clause that adds descriptive detail to a sentence but is not essential for the main idea of the sentence (that is, it can be left out without affecting the main idea). A restrictive modifier, by contrast, is essential to the main idea; it cannot be removed from the sentence without affecting the meaning significantly.

The test to determine whether or not a modifier is restrictive or nonrestrictive is to try removing it from the sentence. If its removal changes the meaning significantly, then the modifier is restrictive and no commas should be used around it. If the removal of the modifier does not alter the main point of the sentence, then the modifier is nonrestrictive and requires punctuation; typically, it is set off by commas, although a pair of parentheses or dashes is sometimes used.

Notice the important difference in meaning between the members of each of the following pairs of sentences (which differ only by the addition of one comma).

> I dislike all students who are lazy.
>
> I dislike all students, who are lazy.
>
> Repair all the old computers which are broken.
>
> Repair all the old computers, which are broken.

In the first sentence of each pair (with no commas), the modifier is restrictive; that is, it restricts the meaning of the word it describes to a certain group (to lazy students, and to the broken computers). In the second member of each pair (with commas), the phrase does not restrict the meaning of the word it modifies, so the sentence refers to all students, and all old computers. If one removes these nonrestrictive modifiers from the second pair of each sentence, the main point of the sentence remains the same; only some additional descriptive detail is missing. But one cannot remove the modifier in the first sentence of each pair without seriously affecting the meaning.

3.23 | Whether a particular phrase or clause is restrictive or nonrestrictive depends upon the meaning the writer wishes to convey. Grammatically speaking, the presence or absence of punctuation does not mean the sentence is not complete and independent. But there can be a significant change in meaning from one version to the other.

3.24 | The above rule about no punctuation around restrictive modifiers applies particularly to titles of works and to names. Names and titles are sometimes restrictive and sometimes nonrestrictive, depending on the context. If the name of the work or the person is essential to the identification of what you are talking about, then the title or the name is restrictive, and it should not be set off by punctuation. If the name or the title is not essential, put commas around it.

> In Ibsen's play *A Doll's House*. . . .
> [The title is restrictive here, because Ibsen wrote many plays; we need the specific title to identify which one the writer is talking about; thus, do not use punctuation around the title.]
>
> Prime Minister Clark's wife, Mila, visited. . . .
> [The name is nonrestrictive, unless Clark has many wives and we need to know which one the writer is talking about.]
>
> My brother Tom is visiting.
> [No comma here because the writer has three brothers, so the name is essential to the sentence.]
>
> My eldest brother, Tom, is visiting.
> [The name here is non-essential because there can only be one eldest brother; hence, the person is fully identified without the name.]

3.25 | When there are several antecedents before a restrictive relative clause, a comma must precede it; and commas must be used when there are several relative clauses relating to a single sentence. An antecedent is a word, phrase, clause, or sentence to which another word (especially a relative pronoun that follows it) refers.

> There were present men, women, and children, who witnessed the carnage in Aleppo, Syria.
>
> He pointed out to me the three men, Adams, Jackson, and Smith, who were responsible for the robbery.
>
> Politicians, whose ambition is great, whose integrity is often dubious, and whose motivations may be questionable, are hardly "public servants" these days.

3.26 | Dependent clauses are generally separated from the rest of the sentence in which they occur, most of the time using the comma.

> Be his motives what they may, he must soon divulge his true intentions.
>
> This relation of your army to the crown will, if I am not mistaken, become a serious dilemma in your politics.

Of course, this rule must be qualified by the rules for the stronger points, especially the semicolon and colon. It is sometimes necessary to separate the clause from the rest of the sentence by a strong point.

EXCEPTIONS:

No point is needed if either the dependent clause or the main clause is short.

> He would be shocked if he were to know the truth.

But if the dependent clause is inserted parenthetically, it is set off by commas (or stronger marks, if appropriate), however short it may be.

If the sentence in the previous example were inverted, a comma would be used after the dependent clause.

> If he were to know the truth, he would be shocked.

In the first form of this example, *he would be shocked* is a definite, finished statement, the necessary qualification to which should follow with as little pause as possible. But in the inverted form, the first part of the sentence—*if he were to know the truth*—is not a finished statement, and the mind may pause for a moment before going on to the consequence, knowing that a consequence must follow.

3.27 | Use a comma to separate dependent clauses and conditional clauses introduced by such words as *if, when, though,* unless the connection is close.

> He did not stop, though I called repeatedly.
>
> Your solution is right in method, even if you have made a mistake in the work.

3.28 | Dependent clauses placed before the main clause usually have a comma separating them from the independent clause to mark the start of the main idea (unless the introductory material is very short and sometimes even then). Similarly, dependent clauses that come after the main clause are separated from the main clause by a comma unless the dependent clause is restrictive. In the following examples, the dependent clauses are underlined and followed by a comma.

> <u>When we returned</u>, we found the materials in disarray.
>
> <u>Since it is raining</u>, I am going back to the office, where I shall work until 6:00 p.m.

In the above sentence, the introductory dependent clause (*Since it is raining*) has a comma between it and the start of the main idea. Likewise, a comma is used between the end of the main idea and the dependent clause at the end (*where I shall work until 6:00 p.m.*).

3.29 | When one sentence depends in sense upon another, this dependence being often expressed by a conjunction denoting cause or result, or by an adverb denoting time, the sentences should be separated by a comma.

> Rob not the poor, because he is poor.
>
> Whoever rewards evil for good, evil shall not depart from his house.
>
> Wherever we are, we are never beyond the watchful eye of the government.
>
> Go where you will, you will never find a place so dear to yourself as your own home.

3.30 | Do not insert a single comma into the middle of a clause (between the subject and the verb or between the verb and its object), unless there is a specific requirement for it. In most cases, you will need to insert a pair of commas, rather than just one.

> ✗ The frequency of urban crime, is an urgent concern.
>
> ☺ The frequency of urban crime is an urgent concern.

The comma is incorrect in the above sentence as it is first written because it breaks the continuity between the subject and the verb.

3.31 | Use a comma to set off words or phrases that express contrast.

> Mr. Fong, not Mr. Adams, won the election.
>
> The weather was cloudy, not typical of a summer day in July.
>
> We rule by love, not by force.
>
> The man was tall, yet shorter than others on his sports team.

In the following example, the phrase *not long after they married* does not contrast with the first part of the sentence; it adds information to the statement, so no comma is required.

> She pushed her husband off the bridge not long after they married.

You may omit a comma that sets off a contrasting phrase that begins with *but*, if you wish. The following sentences are both correct:

> ☺ His wife was quiet but visibly angry.
>
> ☺ His wife was quiet, but visibly angry.

3.32 | Use a comma after an interrogative clause when it is followed by a direct question.

> You will call me, won't you?
>
> You are healthy, are you not?
>
> You will go to the picnic, will you not?
>
> Just shut up, will you please?

3.33 | Do not put a comma after a verb of speaking unless you are indicating a direct quotation, and then a comma (or a colon to introduce a longer quotation) is required.

> ✗ She said "I killed the victim."
>
> ☺ She said, "I killed the victim."

✗ She said, that she killed the victim.
☺ She said that she killed the victim.

☺ Lincoln declared: "Four score and seven years ago our fathers brought forth on this continent, a new nation, conceived in Liberty…"

3.34 | When a comma is used with quotation marks, it is always placed inside the closing mark. The same rule usually applies to a period, question mark, and exclamation mark; but a few exceptions are discussed later in the chapter on quotation marks.

"Honesty is the best policy," as the proverb says.

The items marked "A," "B," and "C" were listed in the ad.

She promised "four," not "five."

3.35 | Where there is no danger of obscurity, the subject must not be separated from the predicate by a comma or other punctuation.

The prestige of your position gave you an exaggerated sense of your own importance.

3.36 | When the subject is long, a comma may be placed after it for clarity. The reader's eye at once observes the separating point.

To say that he endured without a murmur the misfortune that came upon him, is to say only what his previous life would have led us to expect.

When the subject is long, and it is itself separated by commas, it is best to insert a comma before the verb. But this is a matter of judgement, based on how the sentence reads with and without the comma.

The love of money influencing us in our daily actions to the exclusion of the motives of a common interest and humanity, is certain to work to our injury.

The time of difficulty, of trial, of temptation, came upon them unexpectedly.

> That an immense ship could be sailed across the Atlantic between Liverpool and New York in the short period of six days, would not have been believed by the ancients.

Whether the subject is short or long, however, if it ends in a verb, a comma is usually placed after it.

> The good that men do, lives after them.
>
> Whoever breathes, lives.
>
> Those who will confess, may live.

3.37 | If a word is repeated for the sake of emphasis, a comma follows it each time that it occurs; but, in the case of an adjective repeated before a noun, no comma is used after the last expression of it.

> It was work, work, work, from morning till night.
>
> He travelled a long, long way.
>
> Truly, truly, this is a sad occurrence.

3.38 | Words used in pairs must be separated from the rest of the sentence by commas.

> Sink or swim, live or die, survive or perish, I am for the declaration.
>
> Young or old, male or female, rich or poor, everyone must pay taxes.

3.39 | When words are common to two or more parts of a sentence, and are expressed only in one part, a comma is often used to show that they are omitted in the other parts.

> London is the capital of England; Paris, of France; Berlin, of Germany.

Though some writers often punctuate contracted sentences in this way, it is better not to insert the comma when the meaning is equally clear without it. It is unnecessary in the following sentence:

> ✗ Saul has slain his thousands, and David his ten thousands.
>
> ☺ Saul has slain his thousands and David his ten thousands.

3.40 | Use the comma to set off any sentence element that is placed out of its natural order.

> If it is possible, he will do it.
>
> To most people, this will seem absurd.

3.41 | Use the comma to separate words, clauses, and sentences that are so closely connected as to preclude the use of the colon or semicolon and yet require some point to limit or introduce a pause into the meaning. In general, if the meaning passes on efficiently from one word to those that follow without a break in the sense, no comma or other punctuation mark is required.

> "The laws of chivalry compelled him to be true to his word."

No break in the sense occurs in this sentence; no comma is required.

> "The laws of chivalry," says Carlyle, "compelled him to be true to his word."

Here the break is plainly evident, as is the necessity for the commas; as also in the following:

> The laws of chivalry, in that day, compelled the knight to be true to his word.
>
> Persuade, urge, encourage him to do his best.
>
> Although genius always commands admiration, character most commands respect.
>
> Johnathan, who was the oldest and strongest of the brothers, lived to a very old age.
>
> In youth we lay the foundation, in adult years we build the structure, of a life.

3.42 | When the words *as* and *than* connect dependent sentences, a comma is not usually required. But when two correlative conjunctions are used in dependent sentences, like *so and as, though and yet,* the comma is more frequently employed to separate them, unless the sentences are short.

We are never better satisfied <u>than</u> when we are allowed to have our own way.

They are wiser <u>than</u> we ever hope to be.

We shall be <u>as</u> they are now.

<u>As</u> the autumn leaves fall, <u>so</u> we prepare for the coming winter.

<u>Though</u> he is not a nice man, <u>yet</u> he strives to be fair.

3.43 | When writing the word *too* in a sentence, commas may be used or not at the writer's discretion; either is correct. Some style books suggest that using the comma puts slightly more emphasis on the word *too*.

☺ I like it too.

☺ I like it, too.

3.44 | Use the comma whenever there is a distinct pause in the sentence for any reason that is not otherwise indicated by punctuation, or whenever something clearly is omitted.

We want students, not children who simply come to school.

Cæsar had his Brutus; Charles the First, his Cromwell;

3.45 | The difference between writing two commas, two brackets, or two dashes around a nonrestrictive modifier is mainly a matter of emphasis. The most common practice is to use two commas. Do not use dashes unless you want to create a special emphasis.

3.46 | Always put a comma after *e.g.* and *i.e.* if you use these abbreviations at all, and as stated in an earlier chapter, it is better to avoid them; instead, write *for example* or *that is*.

Correct: I like ethnic food (e.g., Thai, Mexican, and Indian).

Preferred: I like ethnic food (for example, Thai and Indian).

Correct: The year has four seasons, i.e., winter, spring, summer, and fall.

Preferred: The year has four seasons, that is, winter, spring, summer, and fall.

Preferred: The year has four seasons—winter, spring, summer, and fall.

3.47 | Do not use a comma before an ampersand (&), even in a list of words in which you would typically use a serial comma.

✗ Smith, Wesson, & Co.

☺ Smith, Wesson & Co.

3.48 | Omit commas wherever you can do so without creating ambiguity or confusion in your sentences.

Executive Order No. 21

Public Law 85-1

He graduates in the year 2016. (never write *2,016*)

My age is 30 years 6 months 12 days.

John Lewis II

Murphy of New York (where only last name is used)

3.49 | Use a comma to indicate an ellipsis if using an ellipsis would disrupt the flow of the sentence.

Subscription for the course, fifty dollars.

Very brief sentences, especially in advertising copy, are exceptions to this rule and the comma should be omitted:

Tickets 50 cents

Price ten dollars

Numbers and Dates

3.60 | Writing and punctuating numbers and dates is a source of confusion for many writers and even editors, in part because various style guides offer conflicting advice. In AP Style, you should write out whole numbers up to and including nine, and use digits for numbers over nine. (*Mary has four sons and 13 cats.*) Likewise, use digits for measurements (*2 cups, 12 ounces, 50 pounds, 4 feet, 65 mph*); but spell out numbers in casual expressions (*A picture is worth a thousand words.*).

Chicago Style, by contrast, recommends that you spell out whole numbers up to and including one hundred; write digits for amounts greater than one hundred (*zero, six, ninety-nine, 101, 1,000*), and for measurements (*1 cup, 5 yards, 150 pounds*). Write out whole numbers up to and including one hundred when followed by hundred, thousand, million, billion, trillion, etc. (*five hundred* but *506; six hundred thousand; one million; twenty billion*). But an "alternate rule" for handling numbers was recently introduced in Chicago Style. For the most part, it mirrors AP Style: spell out whole numbers up to and including nine, and use digits for everything else. The choice is left to the writer's judgement, but whichever rule you follow, you must remain consistent throughout your manuscript. Don't switch back and forth from one style to the other, as this will give your writing a sloppy, unedited quality and could confuse the reader.

3.61 | Use a comma to set off thousands and millions when numbers over 999 are written as digits.

> Having 4,230 website hits is good, but 1,500,000 hits is better.
>
> He won the election by a razor-thin margin of 82,614 votes.
>
> China's population hit 1,382,106,527 at midnight on June 17, 2016.

3.62 | Always spell out a number at the beginning of a sentence, or rewrite the sentence to avoid awkward construction.

> ✗ 30 people were left homeless as a result of the storm.
>
> ☺ Thirty people were left homeless as a result of the storm.
>
> ✗ 2017 is likely to be a volatile year in US politics.
>
> ☺ The year 2017 is likely to be volatile in US politics.

✗ $5,000 is the amount she lost on that failed stock investment.

☺ Five thousand dollars is the amount he lost on that failed stock investment.

☺ He lost five thousand dollars on that failed stock investment.

3.63 | When two numbers appear in apposition, or side by side, whether they are spelled out as words or written as digits, use a comma to separate them if the meaning of the sentence would be unclear or awkward without the comma. Notice in the below examples marked as incorrect how the numbers written side by side are confusing or don't flow well without the comma that has been inserted in the correct examples.

✗ Instead of hundreds thousands joined the protest.

☺ Instead of hundreds, thousands joined the protest.

✗ Instead of fifty 350 prisoners escaped from the Brazilian prison.

☺ Instead of fifty, 350 prisoners escaped from the Brazilian prison.

✗ December 7 1941

☺ December 7, 1941

✗ In 2016 800 people fell ill with the disease.

☺ In 2016, 800 people fell ill with the disease.

✗ When the clock struck midnight 180 missile were launched on enemy targets.

☺ When the clock struck midnight, 180 missiles were launched on enemy targets.

3.64 | Spell out ordinal numbers up to and including hundredth in Chicago Style (*Jane's first impression, seventy-fifth, 200th*). In AP

Style, spell out ordinals up to and including ninth, and write larger ordinals as digits (*first, sixth, 12th, 75th*). But use digits when indicating sequence in naming conventions, such as *4th U.S. Circuit Court of Appeals.*

3.65 | Don't use commas in fractions, decimals, street addresses, telephone numbers, or serial/registration numbers (except patent numbers).

> 1/1500
>
> 5.1947
>
> page 2632
>
> Part No. 189463
>
> 805-555-1212
>
> 1721-1727 Main Street
>
> 6,763,901 B1 (patent number)

3.66 | Do not use a comma before or within a ZIP code designation.

> Santa Barbara, CA 93101
>
> East Rochester, OH 44625-9701

3.67 | Do not use a comma before abbreviated compass directions.

> 1216 North Sunset Drive NW

3.68 | Use the four-digit number to express calendar years. Never use a comma or spell out the year.

> ✗ The man time-traveled to the year three thousand BCE.
>
> ☺ The man time-traveled to the year 3000 BCE.
>
> ✗ August 2,016
>
> ☺ August 2016

Because a sentence must not begin with a number, and calendar years must be expressed in digits, you might have to rewrite your sentence and place the date somewhere other than at the beginning.

The Comma | 51

✗ 2,016 was a contentious year in US politics.
[Do not use a comma in a calendar year.]

✗ 2016 was a contentious year in US politics.
[Spell out a number when it starts a sentence.]

✗ Twenty sixteen was a contentious year in US politics.
[Awkward construction, doesn't flow well.]

☺ Without a doubt, 2016 was a contentious year in American politics.

☺ The year 2016 was contentious in American politics.

3.69 | Omit the comma in dates written as month and year, holiday and year, season and year, and with European date format.

June 2015

Labor Day 2016

February and March 2016

Easter Sunday 2016

5 January 2006

Summer 2016

The weather for May 2016 was fairly close to normal.

The 10 April 2016 registration deadline has passed.

3.70 | Use a comma after the day and year in a complete date that uses month-day-year format when written in a sentence.

The dates of May 20, 2016, to June 22, 2016, were reserved.

This fact was mentioned in the June 13, 2007, report.

Names, Titles, and Locations

3.80 | When a noun or a phrase in direct address begins the sentence, place a comma after it. When a noun or a phrase in direct address falls in the middle of the sentence, set it off with commas before and after.

Officer, was I driving too fast?

> No, Doris, I do not remember.
>
> Kevin, you frightened me!
>
> Mr. Smith, I will not answer your dumb question.
>
> Yes, Mr. Webb, I will re-schedule the meeting.

3.81 | Use a comma between the title of a person and the name of an organization if the words *of* or *of the* are not used.

> managing partner, Luna Technology Inc.
>
> president, University of California
>
> president of the University

Notice that the third example includes the words *of the,* so no comma is needed here.

3.82 | Omit the comma before name suffixes such as Jr., Sr., Esq., PhD, Inc., and so on, even if the comma is part of the name. But add a comma after a name suffix when it is followed by a title or when other rules apply that would require a comma.

> John Ryan Jr., chairman of the committee, just gave a speech. [but John Ryan Jr. is chairman of the committee.]
>
> Allan Wilson III, London resident, drove his car into the river. [but Allan Wilson III drove his car into the river.]
>
> Motorola Inc. factory workers are entitled to overtime.
>
> Smith, A.H., Jr. (not Smith Jr., A.H.)
>
> Juan Garcia II was elected local sheriff.
>
> Mr. Combs Jr. also spoke.

3.83 | Use a comma when a full name or a title and a name are followed by an organization or location.

> James Adam Cullen, of Los Angeles
>
> President Faust, of Harvard University
>
> Dr. Judy Greenberg, of Holy Cross Hospital

3.84 | Use a comma between a person's name and his title or degree.

> Allan West, Chief Executive Officer
>
> Sarah W. Eliot, PhD
>
> Rev. Mark McCafferty, Pastor

When a name and title are written mid-sentence, don't forget the second comma. Also note that the title or other additional information can be set off by parentheses or em dashes rather than commas, depending on whether emphasis is desired.

> **No emphasis on job title:**
>
> ☺ John Smith, technology director, issued the regulations.
>
> **Some emphasis:**
>
> ☺ John Smith (technology director) issued the regulations.
>
> **More emphasis:**
>
> ☺ John Smith—technology director—issued the regulations.

3.85 | Don't use a comma between a person's name and a location when the person is closely identified with the place.

> Joan of Arc
>
> Henry of Navarre

3.86 | Use a comma before the word *of* when a proper name is connected with the person's residence or position.

> Senator Lodge, of Massachusetts
>
> Professor Smith, of Cal State Northridge

3.87 | Separate the parts of an address or a geographical location with commas when you include those details in a sentence.

> He lived at 206 Westfield Street, Boston, MA, for many years.

3.88 | When you write out the address at the top of a business letter or on the envelope, do not put commas or any other punctuation at the end of each line.

>   Microsoft Corporation
>   One Microsoft Way
>   Redmond WA 98052

3.89 | Use a comma after the salutatory phrase at the beginning of a letter, when the salutation is informal (typically, a first name is used). If the salutation is formal, as in a business letter, then use a colon.

> **Informal:**
>
> Dear John,
>
> Hey Betty,
>
> Yo dude,
>
> **Formal:**
>
> Dear Sir:
>
> To Whom It May Concern:
>
> Dear Mrs. Smith:
>
> Ladies and Gentlemen:

3.90 | Use commas to separate the closing salutation of a formal letter from the rest of the sentence of which it forms a part.

>   Anticipating your prompt response, I am,
>   Very truly yours,
>   John Q. Smith

3.91 | Do not use a comma in bibliographies between the publication name and volume or issue number. But use a comma before the date, if one is listed:

>   Library of Congress Bulletin 34:238
>
>   Library of Congress Bulletin 34:238, April 2016

Chapter 4

The Semicolon

> "I use a whole lot of half-assed semicolons; there was one of them just now; that was a semicolon after 'semicolons,' and another one after 'now.'"
>
> Ursula K. Le Guin

Semicolons, like commas, are often used incorrectly by writers and English grammar learners who haven't mastered the basics of punctuation. Now that you've acquainted yourself with the rules of comma usage, we will go on in this chapter to explore the rules for using the semicolon in modern writing.

The semicolon denotes a degree of separation, or a pause, greater than that of the comma, but less than that of the colon or a full stop. It can help to set off important words in a sentence and enhance readability of complex phrases, especially phrases marked with commas, that would otherwise be ambiguous or difficult for readers to follow. Used correctly, the semicolon can help you to avoid overuse of commas. It also allows for greater variation in sentence structure and a more interesting writing style than is possible if you rely primarily on commas and full stops.

One of the most common uses of the semicolon is to connect two or more independent clauses or word groups together in a longer sentence to express a complete thought before the sentence ends with a full stop. Semicolons have other uses in shorter sentences and word groups too.

4.01 | A semicolon can be used to separate two independent clauses in a compound sentence. When used in this way, the semicolon has the same utility as a full stop. Therefore, don't use it except where a full stop would be equally correct; that is, do not create sentence fragments.

> ☺ Kevin purchased a silver Lexus; the luxury sedan has many high-end features.

If we replace the semicolon in the above sentence with a full stop, the passage still makes sense, which confirms that we have used the semicolon appropriately.

> ☺ Kevin purchased a silver Lexus. The luxury sedan has many high-end features.

4.02 | Don't use the semicolon to separate unequal parts of a sentence, such as to separate an opening subordinate clause from a main clause. Instead, use a comma in such constructions.

> ✗ Although he loves Melinda; Jason does not understand her.
>
> ☺ Although he loves Melinda, Jason does not understand her.
>
> ✗ While waiting for the bus; Mark was robbed by two thugs.
>
> ☺ While waiting for the bus, Mark was robbed by two thugs.

In the incorrect examples above, if you replace the semicolon with a full stop, you will turn the first phrase into a fragment. To rectify the mistake, replace the semicolon in each sentence with a comma.

Remember that when a semicolon is used to connect two independent clauses in a compound sentence, you'll be able to replace the semicolon with a conjunction and still have a correctly written sentence. A conjunction forms a bridge over the gap between two statements, and, when both are short and uncomplicated, we read from one to the other without noticing a distinct break. But if you desire a more prominent break, a stronger point is required, and the semicolon fulfills this need.

4.03 | A semicolon can be used to separate two or more items in a list.

Some writers use a computer; others who long for the old-fashioned romance of writing use a typewriter; still others, for a variety of reasons, prefer to write with a pencil or a pen.

The pretty brunette wore a sheer black top; a tight-fitting black skirt; four-inch stiletto heels; and she carried a bright red umbrella that didn't go with her outfit.

4.04 | Use a semicolon, rather than commas, where one or more of the items in a list include commas, and using additional commas in the sentence would create ambiguity or confusion.

✗ Comma confusion:
The wealthy businessman owns homes in Miami, Florida, Las Vegas, Nevada, and Aspen, Colorado.

☺ Preferred, use semicolons to separate list items:
The wealthy businessman owns homes in Miami, Florida; Las Vegas, Nevada; and Aspen, Colorado.

✗ Comma confusion:
Rallies were held in Chicago, Detroit, and Springfield on January 21, in Denver on January 22, and in San Francisco, Los Angeles, and San Diego on January 23.

☺ Preferred, use semicolons to separate list items:
Rallies were held in Chicago, Detroit, and Springfield on January 21; in Denver on January 22; and in San Francisco, Los Angeles, and San Diego on January 23.

4.05 | Similarly, use a semicolon to separate the parts of a compound or a complex sentence other than list items, when those parts contain commas.

☺ As solders, we admire the courageous warrior; but, as brave soldiers, we do not admire the soldier who cowers on the battlefield.

☺ He spends his money for movies, dinners, and wine; and for his family he has not a cent.

4.06 | A semicolon may be used to replace a period and combine two short, distinct, and closely related sentences into a single thought.

> I bought a new car; it is red with a black interior.
>
> His book contained typos; he didn't bother to proofread it.
>
> Don't apologize; you obviously aren't sorry.
>
> Call me in the morning; you can let me know then.
>
> Eat your dinner; I spent two hours cooking it.
>
> Susan is lousy at math; she failed the exam.

4.07 | When using a semicolon instead of a period to join two independent clauses and emphasize a close relationship between the two clauses, do not capitalize the word after the semicolon unless that word is a proper noun, which normally should be capitalized.

> ✗ The report is on our website; You can download it.
>
> ☺ The report is on our website; you can download it.
>
> ☺ The report is on our website; John and Susan can download it.

4.08 | Use a semicolon before a conjunctive adverb such as *however* or *likewise* when it introduces a complete sentence. In most cases, a comma should be placed after the conjunctive adverb. A list of conjunctive adverbs is included below for handy reference.

> I asked you to stop; however, you kept doing it.
>
> You wrote two novels; likewise, Sue Ellen wrote two thrillers.
>
> Bring potato chips; also, bring sodas and hot dog buns.
>
> George was pleased by the news; indeed, he was ecstatic.
>
> I plan to live forever; of course, that's not likely to happen.
>
> I don't like that plan; in fact, I think it is a stupid idea.

List of conjunctive adverbs

accordingly	hence	namely
again	however	nevertheless
also	in addition	of course
as a result	indeed	otherwise
besides	in fact	still
consequently	in particular	that is
finally	instead	then
for example	likewise	therefore
further	meanwhile	thus
furthermore	moreover	

4.09 | Use the semicolon to separate lengthy clauses of a compound sentence or clauses which are not joined by conjunctions.

> He plans to work full-time for two more years; then he probably will return to college.

4.10 | Use a semicolon before the abbreviated forms of conjunctive adverbs (*viz., i.e., e.g.*) when used to introduce a series of terms, simple in form, which are in apposition with a general term. But it is better to avoid the use of such abbreviations in modern writing (see Rule 2.16).

> In the United States today, only two political parties have any real power; i.e., the Republicans and the Democrats.

4.11 | The semicolon is the mark typically used to separate parts of a sentence too closely connected to be made separate sentences, but when the writer desires a distinct break.

> The young patient began to feel better on Monday; and, perhaps, by Friday, he will be well enough to return to school.

> The author himself is the best judge of his own performance; no one has so deeply meditated on the subject; no one is so sincerely interested in the event.

4.12 | A semicolon can be used to join compound sentences in which the subject of the first clause differs quite a bit from that of the second, and you want to combine them into a single thought.

> Marilyn had a fight with her neighbor; the family that lives across the street never argues with anyone.
>
> The power of England relies upon the wisdom of its statesmen; the power of America upon the strength of its military.
>
> In Maria's novel, an earthquake destroys the West Coast; her husband is afraid of earthquakes and won't read the book.

4.13 | A variation of the preceding rule is to use a semicolon when writing contradictory or contrasting statements that you want to connect and express as one thought.

> No; we received one-third.
>
> It is true in peace; it is true in war.
>
> War is destructive; peace, constructive.

4.14 | Use a semicolon to set off explanatory words that explain or summarize the main thought in the preceding matter.

> The trade organization represents businesses that manufacture peripherals for desktop computer users; for example, keyboards, mice, monitors, and flash drives.
>
> Three hotels in Las Vegas offer hefty discounts on rooms during the hot summer months; namely, the Luxor Hotel, Treasure Island, and the Flamingo.

4.15 | The semicolon can be used to join two short but related independent clauses or phrases to avoid choppiness that would result from writing two sentences.

> Yes, sir; he did see it.
>
> No, ma'am; I do not recall.
>
> Wait a minute; why did you say that?
>
> I stopped running; I had to catch my breath.

4.16 | Use a semicolon to indicate chapter references in Biblical citations.

>John 9:1-12; 12:3-6

>John 9:1-3, 6-12; 12:3-6

4.17 | Can I Use Semicolons in Dialogue?

Using semicolons in dialogue was frowned upon in the past. American author Kurt Vonnegut considered semicolons in general to be bad form and declared: "Do not use semicolons. They are transvestite hermaphrodites representing absolutely nothing. All they do is show you've been to college."

But everything changes over time, including language, as Scottish-American author Gilbert Highet noted: "Language is a living thing. We can feel it changing. Parts of it become old: they drop off and are forgotten. New pieces bud out, spread into leaves, and become big branches, proliferating."

In contemporary writing and publishing circles, some editors don't like semicolons in dialogue and will remove them; but increasingly, this punctuation mark is finding its way into mainstream fiction. Its use today is common enough that it should be left to each writer to decide based on personal preference and the writer's individual style.

The semicolon can add flexibility and interest to the structure of dialogue when used correctly. As with most constructions, however, moderation is good, but overuse is not. Use this punctuation mark sparingly and only where it fits well. Because it is not seen often in dialogue, overuse may be glaringly obvious to some readers and should be avoided.

Chapter 5

The Colon

> "It can be said that the colon is not the period, it is the period of the period, the canceling of the period. It is a moment mute and marked; it is the most delicate tattoo of the text."
>
> — Hélène Cixous

The colon represents a longer stop than a comma or semicolon, and it is roughly equal to a full stop. But rather than indicating the end of a sentence, it joins distinct and related sentences, lists, or phrases into a longer sentence that expresses a single thought. In writing styles of the previous century, the presence of a colon nearly always meant that a sentence was long and complex. That's not necessarily the case today. For contemporary writers, the colon offers some flexibility and can be used in various ways, as the rules in this chapter illustrate.

5.01 | A colon is commonly used to introduce, list, or define something. A colon transforms a sentence into a word equation. It signals that what comes next is directly related to the previous sentence. Thus, use a colon after a complete sentence that introduces a list.

> We have yet to finish three activities: writing, editing, and proofreading the article.

> The exhibit includes photographs and memorabilia from three former US presidents: Bill Clinton, George W. Bush, and Barack Obama.

Note that the words preceding a colon must form a complete sentence. If an introductory phrase begins the sentence, use a comma or a dash instead of a colon.

5.02 | Some style guides state that the word immediately following a colon should be capitalized, if it begins a complete sentence; otherwise, write the word in lowercase.

> ✗ The company is hiring for the following jobs: Secretaries, translators, and sales reps.

> ☺ The company is hiring for the following jobs: secretaries, translators, and sales reps.

> ✗ The professor came to the point: he warned that I will fail the course if I don't study.

> ☺ The professor came to the point: He warned that I will fail the course if I don't study.

Chicago Style takes a different approach, that, is, lowercase the word, unless it begins a complete sentence *and* that sentence begins a series of two or more sentences.

> ✗ The professor came to the point: He warned that I will fail the course if I don't study.

> ☺ The professor came to the point: he warned that I will fail the course if I don't study.

Because the example below includes a colon followed by at least two complete sentences, we would uppercase the word *He*.

> ☺ The professor came to the point: He warned that I will fail the course if I don't study. I must therefore spend another hour or two every day studying.

5.03 | When several items or subjects are listed in a formal manner, and they are introduced by the words *thus, as follows, these,* or the like, place a colon before the subjects.

> Let me call your attention to these three states: California, Oregon, and Washington.
>
> The chemicals detected in the water were as follows: chlorine, iron, and magnesium.

5.04 | When several items are separated by commas and not introduced by any formal word such as *thus or as follows,* and when these items are preceded by an explanatory word such as *namely, that is,* or *as,* a semicolon is commonly used instead of a colon.

> Three qualities are highly desired by many people in life; namely, peace of mind, good health, and financial security.
>
> The word *that* may be used in three different ways; as an adjective, as a relative pronoun, and as a conjunctive adverb.

5.05 | When two simple members of a sentence are not connected by a conjunction, and when the thought is not sufficiently close to permit the use of a comma or a semicolon, a colon may be placed between them. In this case, the latter member generally expresses some inference from the former, or some unexpected wish, conclusion, or statement, based on the statement in the former part of the sentence.

> He took a flight to New York this morning: may he reach his destination without delay or injury.
>
> Skill in writing comes from learning technique and constant practice: great writing typically comes from the study of grammar and style, and the experience of years.
>
> Ask: you will receive.

5.06 | Use a colon to separate two members of a sentence when either or both of the members are subdivided by semicolons.

> Wisdom without innocence is knavery; innocence without wisdom is foolery: be, therefore, as wise as serpents, and innocent as doves.

> The republic may perish; the wide arch of our Union may fall; star by star its glories may expire; stone after stone its columns and its capitol may crumble: but as long as human hearts yearn for liberty, the spirit of America's founding patriots will endure.

5.07 | A colon may be used to introduce a summary statement. Do not use a semicolon for this purpose.

> ✗ The dictator learned something important; brutality has consequences.
>
> ☺ The dictator learned something important: brutality has consequences.
>
> ✗ She came right to the point; the cost overruns must stop.
>
> ☺ She came right to the point: the cost overruns must stop.

5.08 | The colon may be used in proportions.

> concrete mixed 5:3:1

5.09 | A double colon may be used as a ratio sign.

> 1:2::3:6

However, some style guides advise that a colon should not be used to express ratio. In these cases, instead of writing 3:1, write 3-to-1 (as an adjective, as in "a 3-to-1 vote") or 3 to 1 (when the numerals are nouns, as in "odds of 3 to 1"). Refer to the guidelines you are using for your particular project.

5.10 | A colon can be used to formally introduce any matter that completes a full sentence or question.

> One resident of the drought-stricken city asked: What if we run out water?
>
> The question remains: Does the Second Amendment give citizens the right to own machine guns and hand grenades?
>
> The three prerequisites for writing a bestseller are: a great story idea, great writing, and a great marketing plan.

5.11 | Use a colon to introduce a bulleted or numbered list if it is introduced by a complete sentence. Never use a colon after a sentence fragment. Generally, bulleted items within the list should be capitalized only if the item is a complete sentence and ends with a period.

☺ **The introductory clause is a complete sentence.**

The price consumers pay for heating oil can change for a variety of reasons:
- seasonal demand
- fluctuation in crude oil prices
- competition in local markets

✗ **The introduction is not a complete sentence, so the colon is not correct.**

My pets:
- cat
- dog
- bird

5.12 | A colon sometimes separates two main clauses where one might expect a semicolon or a full stop. Normally this occurs only when the second main clause explains or illustrates the first clause.

He was fired for only one reason: he was lazy.

5.13 | Do not put a colon immediately between the verb and its object.

✗ We need: a compass, a flashlight, and a map.

☺ We need the following: a compass, a flashlight, and a map.

5.14 | Do not put a colon immediately after a present participle.

✗ The crew used various tools, including: a pick, a shovel, and several water pumps.

The colon after the word *including* is incorrect here. Either remove it or add the phrase *the following items*, then a colon and the list.

☺ The crew used various tools, including the following items: a pick, a shovel, and several water pumps.

5.15 | Do not put a colon immediately after a preposition.

> ✗ I needed the car for: commuting to work, driving my children to school, and delivering newspapers.

The colon after the word *for* is incorrect. Remove it, or add the phrase *for the following activities*, then the colon and the list.

> ☺ I needed the car for the following activities: commuting to work, driving my children to school, and delivering newspapers.

5.16 | Use a colon to separate the title from the subtitle of a book or article. Write both the title and subtitle in italics if the title refers to a book, or in quotation marks if the title refers to an article in a journal or a chapter in a book.

> *Emotion Recollected in Tranquility: Wordsworth's Lyric Style*
>
> *Crisis in the Far East: The End of Asia's Economic Miracle?*

5.17 | Use colons to separate hours from minutes and minutes from seconds when expressing clock time.

> We met at 2:40 p.m.
>
> 12:00:00 a.m.

5.18 | A reference to a Biblical quotation usually indicates the book, the chapter, and the verse, with a colon separating the chapter number from the verse. In some style guides, a period may be used in place of this colon.

> Genesis 3:12-16 (meaning Genesis, Chapter 3, verses 12 to 16)
>
> Genesis 3.12-16 (strict MLA format)

5.19 | A colon is often used as a separator in other citations as well.

> Journal of Education 3:342-358

5.20 | Put a colon after the salutation at the beginning of a business letter. Do not use a comma here; use a comma after the salutation only in an informal letter.

> **In a business letter—**
> Dear Mr. Anderson:
>
> **In an informal letter—**
> Dear Abby,

5.21 | Avoid using a colon at the very end of a heading in a technical report or at the end of the chapter or section heading in an essay or research paper.

5.22 | When you have a quotation that is at least one complete sentence, you can choose to introduce it with a colon. This option is stronger and more formal than using a comma.

> The geologist reported: "The forecast shows rising natural gas production."

5.23 | Similarly, use a colon before an enumeration, or after a word, phrase, or sentence that constitutes an introduction to something that follows.

> Mr. Royer states in his letter: "You will remember that I promised to send you a copy of my latest musical composition. I am sending it to you today."
>
> There are four essentials of a legal contract: competent parties, consideration, agreement, and legal subject matter.

But sometimes the connection between the introductory words and the quotation may be so close, or the quotation itself may be so short, as to make the comma sufficient.

> He kept repeating to us, "The world has sadly changed."

Short phrases quoted in the course of the sentence need not have any point before them.

> It was a usual saying of his own, that he had "no genius for friendship."

5.24 | A colon may be used to introduce a long, formal quotation, whether it is in your own sentence or set in a paragraph of its own.

> In the opening paragraph, the author describes the farm so as to emphasize the loneliness of the setting: "For miles in every direction, all one could see were brown fields, without the comforting presence of another human habitation."

5.25 | However, when the quotation is long, and when, for the sake of making it more conspicuous, you write it in such a way that it begins another paragraph, a dash may be substituted in place of the colon.

> Ruskin, in his letter on "Traffic," writes as follows—
>
> "A picture of Titian's, a Greek statue, a Greek coin, or a Turner landscape expresses delight in the perpetual contemplation of a good and perfect thing. All delight in art, and all love of it, resolve themselves into simple love of that which deserves love."

5.26 | A colon may be placed after such words and phrases as *again, further, to proceed,* and *to sum up,* when used in marking a new stage in an argument.

> To sum up: if you will agree to the terms I have mentioned, I will sign the agreement.
>
> Let me remind you again: if you cannot say something nice about someone, don't say anything.

5.27 | Use a colon to separate the city of publication from the name of the publisher in bibliographic references.

> *Congressional Directory.* Washington D.C.: U.S. Government Printing Office
>
> *Apocalypse Orphan.* Vancouver: Spectrum Ink Publishing

5.28 | Use a colon in imprints before the year, and include a space on both sides of colon as shown below.

> U.S. Government Printing Office. Washington D.C. : 2015

Chapter 6

The Question Mark

> "A rhetorical question...It has a question mark at the end, but you are not meant to answer it because the person who is asking it already knows the answer."
>
> — Mark Haddon

The question mark, also called an interrogation point, signifies an interrogative clause or phrase. Simply put, it lets the reader know that a question is being asked. It is typically used at the end of a sentence in place of a full stop (period); but it can be used in other ways too, as noted below. We will begin this review of rules pertaining to the question mark with the most common example of how it is used.

6.01 | Use the interrogation point after every direct query to indicate to the reader that a question has been asked.

> Where are you?
>
> Will you vacation in Hawaii this summer?
>
> Elizabeth is missing; have you seen her?
>
> Will you ever grow up?
>
> When the rains move south, do you expect more flooding?

6.02 | A question mark does not necessarily have to fall at the end of a sentence. It can be placed in the middle of a sentence, if the grammatical construction of the sentence requires it.

> ✗ Is he happy, you ask?
>
> ☺ Is he happy? you ask.

6.03 | A sentence may appear to be a declarative statement at first glance but actually be a query that requires an answer and should be punctuated with a question mark.

> You are feeling well today?
>
> I should sign this contract now?
>
> You have been to California?
>
> He really committed the crime?

Similarly, it is fairly common to write a direct question after an affirmative statement, and the resulting sentence requires a terminating question mark.

> "You are happy today, are you not?"
>
> "You will not tell me the truth, will you?"
>
> "You do not know that woman, do you?"

6.04 | An indirect question, or a query implied but not actually asked, is not really a question and should not be followed by a question mark.

> ✗ Mary asked James if he enjoyed his vacation?
>
> ☺ Mary asked James if he enjoyed his vacation.
>
> ✗ Father asked whether I had seen his friend, and how I liked him?
>
> ☺ Father asked whether I had seen his friend, and how I liked him.

If we restore these questions to the direct form, the point of interrogation is required.

> Mary asked, "James, did you enjoy your vacation?"
>
> "Have you seen my friend? How do you like him?" Father asked.

6.05 | When a sentence contains more than one question, sometimes a question mark is placed after each of them, other times only at the end of the sentence. It is placed after each, if each is actually a distinct question, and each query might have a different answer.

> Did he speak in a normal tone? Or shout? Or whisper?

> Do you like dance music? Rock? Country? Classical? Jazz?

In the preceding examples, the person asked might answer yes to one or more of the questions posed, and no to the others.

If a series of questions are cobbled together in a sentence, and the queries are so closely related that a single answer will suffice, then use other punctuation (such as commas or semicolons) to separate the various elements, and place a single question mark at the end of the series.

> ✗ Where are the friends I knew from the Eighties? The all-night partiers? The crazy DJs? The fun-loving bartenders? The great dance clubs where I used to hang out?

> ☺ Where are the friends I knew from the Eighties; the all-night partiers; the crazy DJs; the fun-loving bartenders; the great dance clubs where I used to hang out?

The first example may be written as shown, and it would not be grammatically incorrect; but the question marks scattered throughout the sentence make for choppy reading, so the second construction, which uses semicolons, is preferred. Often, the differences in punctuation are subtle, and whether to use a series of question marks or other appropriate punctuation is left to the writer's discretion.

6.06 | Use a full stop instead of a question mark for an interrogative statement—a declarative sentence that states a fact rather than asks a question. Similarly, use an exclamation point instead of a question mark for an interrogative exclamation that seems to ask a question but actually expresses surprise.

At first glance, interrogative statements and interrogative exclamations seem to be queries; but they are not. Sometimes, a sentence can be written either way at the writer's discretion, and it is up to the writer to punctuate the sentence correctly so that readers grasp the nuanced meaning of the passage. Just as vocal inflections tip off a listener to a speaker's intent, punctuation serves the same function with readers. As the following examples illustrate, the difference can be subtle; but choosing the right punctuation for a particular passage can pack a powerful punch and enhance the quality of your writing.

> How can you expect me to believe you!
> [Interrogative statement; expresses indignation]
>
> How can you expect me to believe you?
> [Asks a question for which an answer is expected]
>
> Will you be shocked when I win the lotto!
> [Interrogative statement; expresses confidence; boasts good fortune is imminent]
>
> Will you be shocked when I win the lotto?
> [Asks a question; an answer is expected]
>
> Why can't I get any peace and quiet around here!
> [Interrogative statement; expresses frustration, possibly annoyance]
>
> Why can't I get any peace and quiet around here?
> [Asks a question; an answer is expected]

6.07 | Similar to the above, an interrogative request is a sentence constructed in such a way that it appears to ask a question, but in reality, it is a specific request or a demand.

> Will you please forward my mail.
> [Interrogatory request; written as an instruction, not a question]
>
> Will you please forward my mail?
> [Asks a direct question]
>
> Would you shut up and let me explain.
> [Interrogatory request; written as a demand, not a question]
>
> Would you shut up and let me explain?
> [Asks a direct question]

The last example is edgy and has a plaintive tone, even when it is expressed as a question; but the writer's use of the question mark here informs the reader that the speaker expects a response and will pause to await it. Contrast this with the first sentence in the pair (interrogatory request), in which the speaker demands that a companion shut up, and the reader expects an explanation to follow.

6.08 | A point of interrogation enclosed within brackets is sometimes used to indicate that there is a doubt whether the statement preceding it is true; whether the expression preceding it is well applied; or that some statement or expression is made or used ironically. Alternatively, the question mark may be enclosed in parentheses. Thus, both forms of this example, the first using brackets, the second using parentheses, are correct.

> ☺ While you are enjoying the delights [?] of downtown Manhattan, I am living in paradise on a sandy beach in California.

> ☺ While you are enjoying the delights (?) of downtown Manhattan, I am living in paradise on a beach in California.

6.09 | A question mark can be used parenthetically to indicate doubt. Enclosing the question mark in parentheses is optional but helps to eliminate confusion about the meaning. When used in this manner, the parenthesis (or question mark on its own) is placed immediately after the word that evokes the doubt, with no space preceding it.

> In 2016(?), David Colby met with an undercover agent in what turned out to be a videotaped sting operation.

> Leonardo da Vinci (1452?–1519)

> Donald met secretly with a woman named Melinda(?) and offered her fifty thousand cash to burn the photographs.

> The statue(?) was on the law books.
> [The writer indicates doubt about the spelling.]

> In 1934(?), Albert Szent-Györgyi discovered Vitamin C.

6.10 | When a direct question is written in quotation marks, a question mark is required at the end, and it must be placed inside the quotation marks.

> The question, "What became of the stolen Picasso?" has never been answered.

> "Why were you out all night?" Sally's mother demanded, practically shouting.

Chapter 7

The Exclamation Point

> "People complain about my exclamation points, but I honestly think that's the way people think. I don't think people think in essays; it's one exclamation point to another."
>
> Tom Wolfe

The exclamation point (or exclamation mark in British English) is used at the end of a word, phrase, or short sentence that expresses surprise or strong emotion (joy, anger, shock, etc.) as with "Hi!" and "Well, that's great!" An uttered expletive is typically followed by an exclamation point. This mark has other uses too, described in this chapter. It has the same effect as a full stop.

The exclamation point dates back to the fifteenth century, when it was used with the Latin word *io*, an exclamation of joy. Until the mid-seventeenth century, it was called the *sign of admiration*. In the 1950s, it was called the *bang*, derived from comic strips that popularized interjections like "POW!" and "ZAP!" The mark did not have its own key on the standard typewriter keyboard until the 1970s; before then, it required typing a period, backspacing, and then typing an apostrophe.

Some writers have expressed contempt for this mark. F. Scott Fitzgerald wrote: "Cut out all these exclamation points...An exclamation point is like laughing at your own joke." But today, it is widely used in casual writing and all genres of fiction. Being that this mark is here to stay, it behooves writers to learn the following rules for its proper use.

7.01 | The exclamation point is used after an expression of great surprise or strong emotion, either positive (delight, pleasure, amazement) or negative (anger, shock, fear, outrage). The expression can be just a syllable, a word, or a short phrase.

> "Look out!" he shouted.
>
> He should be ashamed of himself!
>
> How beautiful!
>
> She groaned, "Oh my God!"
>
> Mayday! Mayday!

7.02 | Avoid using the exclamation point with a compound sentence or with an overly long or complex sentence. If a wordy explanation is needed, rewrite the passage so that the details are separated from the interjection, and reduce the latter to a word or short phrase that expresses the requisite surprise or strong emotion.

> ✗ I received a call from a neighbor informing me that a robber had broken into my house; so I hurried home and found that my computer and TV were gone, and I was so mad!
>
> ☺ I received a call from a neighbor informing me that a robber had broken into my house; so I hurried home and found that my computer and TV were gone. I was so mad!

7.03 | Do not overuse the exclamation point. It is meant to convey surprise or strong emotion. If you end too many sentences with exclamation points, they will lose their impact, and your writing will suffer. Many readers perceive excessive use of exclamation points as being indicative of unpolished, childish, or annoying prose. As a general rule, the exclamation point is rarely used in nonfiction writing.

7.04 | The exclamation point can be used to terminate a short phrase expressed as a wish, a command, or a prayer.

> Leave! Now! Out of my sight!
>
> Heaven help us!

> Wake up!
>
> O Lord, forgive me for what I have done!
>
> I dare you!
>
> If only I could win the lotto!
>
> Stop whining, fool!

7.05 | Where an interjection is repeated without particular emphasis on one element in the series, each may be followed by a comma except the last, which should be terminated with the exclamation point.

> Ha, ha, ha! That's very funny!

7.06 | The mark of exclamation is sometimes placed after an ironical statement.

> They did not fight to defend their wives and children; they did not fight to defend their country, but for vain glory and plunder. They are villains, not heroes!

7.07 | The mark of exclamation can be placed after a statement that reflects irony or some absurdity.

> He is convinced that his neighbor is from another planet!
>
> Don't ask questions if you aren't prepared for the answers!
>
> Life is what you make it!
>
> Freedom of the press is granted to those who are wealthy enough to own a printing press!

7.08 | The mark of exclamation may be placed after any impressive or striking thought.

> Franklin D. Roosevelt once said: "When you see a rattlesnake poised to strike, you do not wait until he has struck to crush him!"

Some editors contend that using an exclamation mark in this way serves no real purpose, since the impressiveness of the sentence ought to be reflected in the sentence itself and not require the writer to add a mark that tells the reader, "This statement is impressive!" Indeed, this touches on the problem of overuse of punctuation marks in general, which all writers should strive to avoid. Punctuation is not intended to save writers the trouble of putting great care and thought into composing grammatically precise sentences.

7.09 | An exclamation point may be placed after words of emphatic and solemn address.

> "Courageous men! The battle is at hand!"
>
> "Father Almighty! Hear our prayer."

7.10 | The mark of exclamation is placed after sentences that appear at a glance to be questions but are, in fact, exclamatory.

> How could he have been so foolish!
>
> What have you done!
>
> Where is your good sense!

These are examples of what we call rhetorical questions. They are not really questions but exclamatory statements made more striking by being put in the form of questions. They are not asked for the sake of receiving a direct answer, but rather, to express strong feelings. Not all rhetorical questions are punctuated in this manner; sometimes, using a question mark is more effective. In each case, the writer must decide whether the sentence would be better cast as a question or as the expression of emotion.

7.11 | When the emotion being expressed is very strong, double exclamation points may be used:

> Stop him!! That man is a murderer!!

7.12 | When a sentence contains more than one exclamation, sometimes the exclamation point is placed only after the last, sometimes it is placed after each of them, the test being whether or not they are in reality, as well as in form, several exclamations.

> All are thus satisfied with the dispensations of Nature! But how few listen to her voice! How few follow her as a guide!

7.13 | When the word *oh* is used, the context determines whether an exclamation point is appropriate. If it is expressed as an acknowledgement, a desire, or an imprecation, as in the first two examples below, do not use an exclamation point. If it reflects surprise or strong emotion, as in the third example, then use the mark.

> Oh David, I just don't know what to say.
>
> Oh, yes. I knew about that.
>
> Oh! What a surprise!

7.14 | When the word *oh* is used in a sentence and the entire statement expresses surprise or strong emotion, write an exclamation point at the end of the sentence.

> Oh, I can't believe you stole my car!
>
> Oh Lord, the ship is sinking!
>
> Oh, you are such a nerd!

7.15 | When an interjection or exclamatory word does not require a complete pause but is somewhat closely connected with the subsequent words, a comma may be placed after it, and the exclamation point be put at the end of the sentence; or, in some cases, the comma may be omitted, and no pause is then required except at the close.

> Alas, my friend, I have only five dollars to my name!
>
> Welcome, noble defenders of your country!
>
> Sad that you drove your car into a tree!

7.16 | An exclamation point enclosed in parentheses can be placed after a word or phrase to denote surprise or contempt (a question mark is similarly used to express doubt as noted in an earlier chapter).

> He read the fake news story on a website (!) and assumed it had to be true.
>
> This college graduate (!) could not write a paragraph without a dozen spelling errors.

7.17 | Two or more exclamation points are sometimes used in humorous and satirical writing to denote great emotion.

>Here comes the man who knows everything!!
>
>If you believe that ridiculous claim, you'll believe anything!!
>
>Spare me the lecture on saving money; I have no money to save!!

Chapter 8

Dashes and Hyphens

> "There is a phase in the life of every copy editor when she is obsessed with hyphens."
>
> Mary Norris

Dashes and hyphens are used commonly as punctuation marks, and more so in writing of the present day than in the past. The marks are similar in appearance but serve different purposes. The hyphen is a shorter mark; it typically links together compound adjectives and breaks long words that don't fit in the available space on a line. The dash is longer; it has two forms, and both are useful. Dashes are conspicuous in print and guide the reader's attention. Using dashes, you can create sentences of varied complexity, adding interest to your writing style as well as enhancing clarity. But first, you must learn some basic rules for using these marks. We will start with rules for the dash, and then go on to discuss hyphens later in this chapter.

Style Rules for Using the Dash

8.01 | The dash has two forms. The *em* dash, or long dash, has a variety of uses, the most common being that it sets apart a group of words from other words in a sentence. The *en* dash, shorter than an em dash but longer than a hyphen, indicates a span or relationship and connects inclusive numbers. The two dashes are not interchangeable. Following is a sentence that uses both forms:

> The nuclear power plant—located at Diablo Canyon in California—will be shutting down, a process expected to take 2–3 years.

Here an em dash is placed after the word *plant*, and a shorter en dash denotes a span of time in the phrase *2-3 years.*

The terms *em dash* and *en dash* have their origins in the width of the letters *m* and *n*. As the former is the wider of the two letters, the em dash is wider than the en dash, and about twice the width of a hyphen.

Some style guides advise that the dash should be used sparingly or not at all, suggesting that the en dash should be replaced with the word *to,* as in *ten to twenty years,* to indicate range, rather than writing *10–20 years*; and brackets or commas should be used in place of the em dash. But in a sentence like the one below, replacing the dashes with a pair of commas clearly doesn't work, because doing so create comma chaos; and using brackets makes the sentence read like an excerpt from a technical handbook, which likely isn't the writer's intent.

> The ingredients of the true hot dog—bun, wiener, relish, mustard, onion, and ketchup—were not available.

Most grammarians agree that the dash has a place in present-day writing. But as is true with any punctuation mark, writers must avoid overusing this mark. If used too frequently, the dash can lead to choppy sentences that readers may find distracting or annoying.

8.02 | On a typewriter or a word processor, no key exists for typing an en dash or an em dash. To write a dash, type a double hyphen (--), which differentiates it from a standard hyphen.

> The materials needed to build the dog house--lumber, plywood, and nails--should cost less than fifty dollars.

Most word processing programs (Microsoft Word, Open Office, and others) will convert a double hyphen to a dash automatically when you type it. In recent versions of Word, when you type a space, followed by two hyphens and then another space, an en dash is inserted automatically. When you type two hyphens without leaving space, an em dash is inserted. You can also type an en dash by pressing the Ctrl key and the hyphen on the number pad. Insert an em dash by pressing Ctrl + Alt and that hyphen.

8.03 | Whether you should add a space before and after the dash (or double hyphen) will depend on which style manual you are following. AP Style requires a space before and after, Chicago Style says no spaces.

> **Chicago Style**
> The ingredients in the recipe—eggs, butter, and milk—are on my shopping list.
>
> **AP Style**
> The ingredients in the recipe — eggs, butter, and milk — are on my shopping list.

For our purposes in this chapter, we will follow Chicago Style in the examples unless otherwise indicated.

8.04 | Use dashes instead of commas when you want to call special attention to a nonrestrictive clause, a list of items, a group of words, or a particular word. This is always a judgment call by the writer.

> Senator Dingus—reversing his position—now supports privatizing Medicare.
>
> Sue Ellen was always lacking what she needed most—money.

8.05 | Dashes may be used in place of commas or parentheses to set off a phrase within the body of a sentence that requires emphasis. But avoid overusing this construction, as dashes are conspicuous, and too many of them will distract readers.

> The weather is terrible—wind, rain, and fog—but we still have to drive home.

8.06 | Use dashes around appositives if the use of commas might cause confusion.

> ✗ Three former Presidents, Bush, Clinton, and Obama, attended the ceremony.

☺ Three former Presidents—Bush, Clinton, and Obama—attended the ceremony.

8.07 | The dash can indicate an abrupt change in construction. But this can take many nuanced forms. For instance, you can use a dash to indicate a sudden interruption in thought.

> "I am pleased to meet you, Captain—what did you say your name is?"

> "The man I met—I refer to him as Captain Jones—was a Russian spy."

8.08 | A dash similarly can be used to indicate an abrupt change in mood or sentiment.

> Many firefighters perished on 9/11—we honor their memory.

> He brags that he is a billionaire—his wife knows he's a poser.

> Have you ever heard—but how could you possibly hear?

8.09 | A phrase expressing strong or contrary actions or emotions can be set off from the surrounding sentence by a pair of dashes.

> She laughs—she cries—no matter what that man does, she loves him deeply.

8.10 | A dash can be used at the end of a series of phrases that depend upon a concluding clause, or where a final clause summarizes a series of ideas.

> Railroads and airplanes, factories and warehouses, wealth and luxury—these are not the pillars of an evolved society.

> Freedom of speech, freedom of worship, freedom of press—these are basic rights promised by the US Constitution.

8.11 | A dash is used after an introductory phrase that leads into subsequent lines and indicates repetition of that phrase.

> I recommend—
>
> > That we submit them for review and corrections;

> That we then accept the corrections; and
>
> That we publish the corrected report.

8.12 | A dash can be used to lead in to a phrase or expression added to an apparently complete sentence but which refers back to some previous part of the sentence.

> She wondered what her father would tweet next—he had a habit of tweeting the unexpected.

8.13 | Use a dash to mark pauses for dramatic or rhetorical effect.

> They make a war and call it—peace.
>
> Life—is what you make it.
>
> You have published four novels—really?
>
> Sometimes I drink coffee—sometimes tea.

8.14 | The dash is used in rhetorical repetition; for instance, where one part of the sentence, such as the subject, is repeated at intervals throughout the sentence, and the rest of the sentence is kept suspended.

> Can you, in Washington—can you, at this moment in time—can you, as the leaders of the House and Senate, vote to privatize Medicare when it clearly benefits so many older Americans?

8.15 | You can use dashes to set off different amplifications of the same statement.

> The madness of what he plans to do—the driving compulsion that he must do it—the horror of the act that he is about to commit—the anger that burns in his soul—all these complicated factors led the gun-toting man to the crime scene that he is about to create at this moment in time.

8.16 | A dash can be used to indicate the unexpected or what is not the natural outcome of what has gone before:

> He walked along the sandy beach for hours looking for the perfect shell and found instead—trash.

8.17 | Use a dash to abruptly terminate a sentence. If the sentence trails off, use an ellipsis instead. Either way, use this construction sparingly, and as a general rule, only in dialogue and fiction narrative.

> Oh my God, I am so upset I could—
> [The thought ends abruptly, so use a dash.]

> I was hoping you would call but...
> [The thought trails off, so use an ellipsis.]

8.18 | A dash can be used to imply without expressing a conclusion.

> She is a brilliant and talented woman but—

8.19 | Use a dash at the end of an interrupted or an unfinished word.

> Help! Someone is break—

> I deleted my profile on Face—

8.20 | Note that when a dash is written at the end of a sentence, a full stop is not added (but see Rule 6.21 below for an exception). It is common, however, to add a question mark or an exclamation point when such a mark is appropriate in the sentence.

8.21 | Use a dash to indicate one or more letters omitted from a word that you prefer not to write out. This is common practice with expletives. When you write one or more dashes in this manner, and if they appear at the end of the last word in the sentence, terminate the sentence with a full stop.

> Gregory is an obnoxious jacka——.

8.22 | The dash can be used to mark faltering or hesitating speech. But note that an ellipsis is more commonly used in contemporary writing to indicate speech or narrative (less commonly) trailing off.

> ☺ Well—I don't know—that is—no, I cannot accept it.

> ☺ Well...I don't know...that is...no, I cannot accept it.

8.23 | A dash can be substituted in place of a conjunctive adverb, such as *accordingly, namely, however,* etc.

> He excelled in three branches—arithmetic, algebra, and geometry.
>
> She promised to do the laundry—she wasn't in the mood and got drunk instead.

8.24 | When the subject of a sentence is of such length or complexity that its connection with the verb may easily be muddled, it is sometimes left hanging in the sentence and its place supplied by some short expression that sums it up. Write a dash after the subject when it is abandoned in this manner.

> Physical Science, including Chemistry, Geology, Geography, Astronomy; Metaphysics, Theology; Economics; Politics and General Literature—all occupied by turn, and almost simultaneously, his constantly active mind.

8.25 | When we place after a quotation the name of the author to whom it is attributed, precede the author's name with a dash.

> "All the world's a stage."—Shakespeare
>
> "Every man's work shall be made manifest."—I Corinthians 3:13
>
> "Maybe everybody in the whole damn world is scared of each other."—John Steinbeck

8.26 | Use a dash preceding a byline or a run-in credit byline, as shown at the bottom of these four lines of verse, preceding the poet's name.

> Lay the proud usurpers low!
> Tyrants fall in every foe!
> Liberty's in every blow!
> Let us do or die!
>
> —Robert Burns

8.27 | The dash is sometimes used in cataloging as a ditto mark.

> Allen, Tim. *Apocalypse Orphan.* Spectrum Ink, 2016

> —*Prisoners of the Game.* Spectrum Ink, 2016
>
> —*Return of Akavasha.* Spectrum Ink, 2016

8.28 | A dash may be used to set off run-in questions and answers in court testimony, and other similar transcripts.

> Q. Did he go?—A. No.

8.29 | Use a dash to define verse references in the Bible as well as page references in books. If the long dash is too conspicuous, the shorter en dash can be used instead. Either way, do not add a space before or after the dash.

> Matt. v: 1—11 or Matt. v: 1–11
>
> See pp. 50—53 or See pp. 50–53

8.40 | The en dash (–) shows a range from one thing to another, usually numbers or dates. As a general rule, you should be able to substitute the word *to* or *and* for an en dash.

> ☺ The party is from 3:00 p.m. to 5:00 p.m.
>
> ☺ The party runs 3:00 p.m.–5:00 p.m.
>
> ☺ Consumption rose 2%–4%
>
> ☺ Consumption rose between 2% and 4%.
>
> ✗ The office party is 3:00 p.m.—5:00 p.m.
> [Incorrect, because an em dash is used]
>
> ✗ Production decreased from 1997-2007.
> [Incorrect, because a hyphen is used]
>
> ✗ Electricity demand ranged between 1--3 MWh.
> [Incorrect, because a double hyphen is used]

8.41 | To denote a gap of time, use either an en dash or a standard hyphen between the two elements, with no space on either side.

> Monday-Friday
>
> 2016-2020

January-June

Style Rules for Using the Hyphen

8.50 | The rules for using hyphens in compound words are somewhat flexible. Compound words frequently have a *hyphen stage* when they are newly combined; then the hyphen disappears as the compound gains widespread use and becomes one word. For example, *on line* became *on-line* and is now *online*.

8.51 | The hyphen (-) is the shortest of the three dash lines. It connects words for clarity, and it is used to divide words on syllables when they do not fit at the end of a line. The hyphen is a distinct punctuation mark. Never use a hyphen in place of a dash, and vice versa. When people say *use a dash*, they almost always mean the longer em dash.

8.52 | Use a hyphen between words when they are combined to modify the word that follows.

>agreed-upon standards
>
>long-term forecast
>
>five-year period
>
>high-level discussion
>
>second-largest producer

8.53 | Don't use a hyphen in compound words when the meaning is clear without the hyphen and the hyphen will not aid readability, or when the underlying meaning of the words is widely known and likely to be understood by the reader.

>child welfare plan
>
>civil rights case
>
>per capita output

8.54 | Use a hyphen between two proper noun compounds when they are combined to modify the word that follows.

>North-South rivalry

African-American history

California-Oregon border

8.55 | Dangling hyphens are required when two or more hyphenated compounds have a common element and this element is omitted in all but the last term.

pro- and anti-competitive practices

long- and short-term forecasts

mid- and late-2000s

service- and technology-oriented businesses

8.56 | When two modifiers appear before a noun and the first is an adverb that ends in *ly*, no hyphen is required because ambiguity is unlikely.

rapidly falling prices

frequently missed deadlines

heavily skewed results

reasonably priced products

8.57 | When two words used as a compound form a non-English phrase, do not use a hyphen.

per capita consumption

bona fide transaction

ex officio member

8.58 | The fact that you hyphenate two words making up a compound in one sentence does not necessarily mean that you should hyphenate the same words whenever they appear together elsewhere. Consider these examples:

I gave the much-loved dog a new home.

The dog that I adopted was much loved.

We use a low-cost fuel.

That fuel is low cost.

It's a day-to-day task.

I take life day to day.

I bought a new air-conditioning unit.

I never use the air conditioning in the winter.

8.59 | In some cases, you should use a hyphen to prevent mispronunciation or ambiguity of a word.

Write:	To avoid confusion with:
pre-position	preposition
re-creation	recreation
re-sorting	resorting
un-ionized	unionized
re-press	repress
re-treat	retreat

8.60 | Sometimes a hyphen may be required to prevent ambiguity in a sentence.

Unclear: The scientist tested a new defect causing gas.

Clear: The scientist tested a new defect-causing gas.

In the second example above, the hyphen makes it clear that the gas is causing defects; the first sentence says that a new defect is causing the gas. Likewise, in the second sentence below, the hyphen clarifies that we are referring to silver jewelry on a cart rather than a jewelry cart painted silver or made of silver.

Unclear: The silver jewelry cart has nice gifts.

Clear: The silver-jewelry cart has nice gifts.

8.61 | Use a hyphen when the number is a descriptor and a modifier.

12-inch ruler

10-minute delay

275-page book

3-to-1 ratio

8.62 | Use a hyphen between the elements of a fraction.

one-thousandth

one-half

two-thirds

three-fourths of an inch

8.63 | Do not use a hyphen to indicate a range. Use an en dash.

☺ 25–30 inches

☺ between 18 inches and 24 inches

✗ 25-30 inches (hyphen is not correct)

8.64 | Do not use a hyphen to mean minus in text. In the following example, the hyphen looks like a dash, not a subtraction sign, which makes the phrase ambiguous.

✗ Imports-exports

☺ Imports minus exports

8.65 | Do not use a hyphen with a civil or military title denoting a single office; but do use a hyphen for a double title.

Examples of a single title (no hyphen):

major general

former president Clinton

Examples of a double title (hyphen required):

secretary-treasurer

treasurer-manager

8.66 | Use a hyphen with the adjectives *elect* and *designate*.

President-elect

ambassador-designate

The most common spelling questions raised by writers and editors involve compound terms, according to *The Chicago Manual of Style*. Sometimes it's difficult to decide which form to use: spell it out as two words (*in the long term* where "long term" is a noun); hyphenate it (*long-term forecast*, where it is adjective); or combine it into one word with no hyphen and no space (as *online, website*). If your style guide does not offer guidance, then a quick search on Google or Bing will help to confirm which spelling is prevalent.

8.67 | Compounds formed with prefixes (*pre, re, non, ex, anti, bi, co, mid, semi*) are normally closed (no hyphen or space) and written as one word, with some exceptions.

8.68 | Use a hyphen with the prefixes listed in Rule 8.67 if the second part of the word is a proper noun (begins with a capital letter).

> non-American
>
> non-OPEC
>
> sub-Saharan
>
> pro-Russian
>
> ex-Marine

8.69 | With frequent use by the public and as time goes by, open and hyphenated compounds tend to become closed, as with *e-mail* to *email, on-line* to *online*.

8.70 | Following is a list of frequently confused compounds and constructions where hyphens should and should not be used. This list is by no means complete and is meant to provide some useful examples.

A-frame cabin	above-target supply
aboveground utility	absent-minded professor
accident-prone child	agencywide
agreed-upon standards	air conditioning
air-conditioning unit	all-city tournament
all-inclusive study	around-the-clock basis
bad-tempered man	belowground lines
Bidirectional	blue-green dress

breakout (not break-out)
brightly-lit room
cap-and-trade legislation
coal-exporting country
computer-aided learning
Copyeditor
Coworker
Database
day-to-day tasks
Decommission
densely-populated area
dual-fired plant
end use
energy-consuming state
English-speaking person
fair-haired woman
fat-free dessert
first-rate accommodations
flat-tax shortfall
four-year-old son
full-length dress
good-looking guy
high-level officials
high-speed line
high-value asset
Homepage
ice-cold beverage
in-depth analysis
inter-island travel

Brent-like crude
camera-ready copy
cathedral-like ceiling
coal-fired generator
coproducer
cost-of-living increase
custom-built car
day-ahead schedule
decision makers
degree days
drought-stricken area
email (not e-mail)
end-use consumption
energy-related legislation
ex-wife
far-reaching influence
feedstocks
five-day vacation
forward-thinking leaders
freeze-offs
full-power days
government-owned land
high-octane fuel
high-spirited child
higher-cost mines
I-beam construction
in depth
in-state
intraregional

Italian-American club
kind-hearted neighbor
large scale
last-minute rush
lead-free paint
Lightbulb
long term
long-term forecast
low-demand hours
Lower 48 states
lower-than-usual demand
market-based pricing
Megabytes
mid-Atlantic region
mid-summer weather
Midcontinent
middle-aged citizens
Midterm
mouth-watering pie
multiple-purpose uses
Multiyear
nationwide
near-term contract
newly discovered resources
nonproducing regions
nonrenewable
nonspecific
off-highway use
offshore

kilowatt-hour
land-use restrictions
large-scale project
late-winter weather
light-year
line-item veto
long-lasting effect
low-cost housing
low-sulfur diesel
lower-cost coal
lump-sum payment
mayor-elect
mid-1990s
mid-June
midcentury
midday
middle-class voters
midweek
muddle-headed fool
multistage
narrow-minded people
near term
never-ending drama
non-OPEC
nonprofit corporation
nonscientific
nonstatistical
offline
old-fashioned ideas

one-month service
one-stop shop
onshore
part time
per capita
per-household consumption
power plant
prerecession
pretax
quick-witted actor
record-breaking performance
run-up
second-half 2015
self-conscious girl
short term
shut down
six-week course
slow-moving traffic
stakeholders
statewide
strong-willed woman
subsalt
systemwide
ten-minute interval
third-party data
thought-provoking report
time-saving techniques
twenty-page report
two-year contract

one-on-one situation
online
onsite
part-time employees
per household
policymaker
preexisting
preregister
quick-thinking fireman
re-export
reopen
second half
second-largest increase
self-contained units
short-term outlook
shut-down mode
sixty-five-year-old man
smaller-volume producers
state-of-the-art technology
stockbroker
substrata
sugar-free candy
T-square
third-largest producer
third-quarter prices
three-second delay
twentieth-century technology
two-hour seminar
U.S.-owned property

ultra-low radiation	up front
up-front money	up-or-down vote
up-to-the-minute	user-generated data
V-formation	vertically integrated utilities
web page	website
well-behaved children	well-educated people
well-made clothes	wellhead
widely-recognized expert	winter-grade gasoline
world-class agency	world-famous athlete
worldwide inflation	X-ray
year-on-year increase	

8.71 | Use the hyphen when a word must be divided at the end of a line. Always put the hyphen at the end of the first line, not at the beginning of the second, and never divide words except at the end of a syllable.

✗ int-end, prop-ose, superint-endent, expre-ssion

☺ in-tend, pro-pose, superin-tendent, expres-sion

8.72 | Never divide words of one syllable (*though, through, ground*), and do not divide short words (*also, over, into,* and the like).

8.73 | In general, avoid dividing a word in such a way that a syllable of three or fewer letters is written on one line or the other.

✗ ex-pression, talk-ing, il-luminate

☺ expres-sion, talking, illu-minate (or illumi-nate)

8.74 | When one syllable of a word ends with a vowel, and the next syllable begins with the same vowel, hyphenation rules vary between style guides. AP Style advises hyphenation of these compounds; for example, *re-establish, re-renter.* For words beginning with the prefix *co,* AP Style requires the hyphen when forming nouns, adjectives, and verbs indicating status or occupation: *co-author, co-chairman, co-*

defendant, co-host, co-owner, co-partner, co-pilot, co-signer, co-sponsor, co-worker, but use no hyphen in other combinations as *cooperate, cooperative, coeducation, coexist, coexistence, coordinate, coordination, coequal.*

By contrast, Chicago Style says that compounds formed with prefixes should normally be closed, whether they are nouns, adjectives, verbs, or adverbs, although some exceptions apply. One exception is to use a hyphen if its omission would create a word that might in turn cause a misreading of the intended meaning. For instance, *re-creation* versus *recreation, re-mark* versus *remark.*

8.75 | As a rule, a hyphen should not be placed after a simple prefix: *contravene, preternatural, hypercritical, bilateral.* But there are exceptions to this rule: *anti-immigrant, ultra-liberal, semi-lunar.* In these words, the pronunciation is more clearly marked by inserting the hyphen.

8.76 | When a number is spelled out in words rather than written as digits, the words making up the number, if more than one word, are in certain cases separated from each other by a hyphen. This rule applies to the cardinal and the ordinal numbers from twenty-one and twenty-first to ninety-nine and ninety-ninth inclusive. Whether a number should be spelled out or written as a digit is determined by your style guide and is beyond the scope of this book, which focuses on punctuation.

Chapter 9

The Ellipsis

> "*I want to change my punctuation. I long for exclamation marks, but I'm drowning in ellipses.*"
>
> Isaac Marion, *Warm Bodies*

The ellipsis is a punctuation mark that consists of three periods, or points. For example, this is an ellipsis . . . and it can be used in various ways. *Ellipsis* is a word from ancient Greek that means "falling short; omission" (the plural form is ellipses). Common uses of this punctuation mark in modern writing are to express: an unfinished thought; dialogue trailing off; a slight pause; an awkward silence; or a feeling of mystery. Some writers confuse the ellipsis with the dash, which indicates a more sudden interruption. The correct uses of the ellipsis are fairly straightforward and explained in the rules below.

9.01 | An ellipsis consists of three points written with a space between each, or set flush with no spaces. The appropriate format is determined by your style guide. If you add spaces between the points, then use non-breaking spaces (an option available in most word processing software) to prevent the points from breaking onto the next line. Also, your style guide may instruct you to add a space before and after the ellipsis. If you use a closed ellipsis (set flush with no spaces), then the ellipsis is written in the same manner as you would write a dash.

> **Chicago Manual of Style (open ellipsis):**
> So . . . have you heard from James yet?
>
> **Chicago Manual of Style (closed ellipsis):**
> So...have you heard from James yet?

AP Style:
So ... have you heard from James yet?

In *Elements of Typographic Style,* Robert Bringhurst dismisses the open ellipsis as a "Victorian eccentricity. In most contexts, the [open] ellipsis is much too wide." He recommends using the closed ellipsis (no spaces) or the generic ellipsis character available in modern word processing programs, which is the preference of most writers. The examples provided in this chapter conform to Chicago Style unless otherwise noted and are typical of how ellipses are used, particularly in fiction writing.

9.02 | Use an ellipsis to indicate that part of a quotation has been left out. If a politician's exact words were, *"The American people are smarter than my Aunt Sallie's mule and can't be fooled forever,"* and you omit the colorful comparison, then you would write: He said, *"The American people...can't be fooled forever."*

9.03 | Alternatively, three asterisks may be used instead of the ellipsis to mark an omission from a sentence or paragraph. In the following speech by John F. Kennedy on "The Long View of the World," two sentences have been omitted, and the asterisks alert the reader:

> "This has been a week of momentous events around the world. The long, painful struggle in Algeria drew nearer to solution. Both nuclear powers and neutrals labored at Geneva to renew the quest for disarmament. * * * And my wife had her first and last ride on an elephant."

9.04 | If the passage omitted is of considerable length, as for instance a complete paragraph, or if a line of poetry is omitted, the asterisks are placed on a line by themselves.

There is a tendency to use the asterisk only to denote lengthy omissions, and to use the ellipsis for shorter omissions. If a complete sentence, or more, is omitted, and the writer elects to use an ellipsis to mark it, the number of points to be used is generally four rather than three. But if a passage is omitted in the middle of a sentence and consists of a shorter phrase, the number is generally three.

9.05 | Regardless of the ellipsis style you prefer, be consistent. Do not use an open ellipsis in one paragraph and a closed ellipsis in the next paragraph. Choose a style and use it consistently from the first page to the last page of your project.

9.10 | If a clause or phrase ends with an ellipsis, and it is a complete sentence that takes a question mark or exclamation point, put the ellipsis before the punctuation in Chicago Style. For AP Style, place the terminating question mark at the end of the sentence, follow it with a space, and then the ellipsis, as in the third example below.

> **Closed Ellipsis:**
> How could you...?
>
> **Open Ellipsis:**
> How could you . . . ?
>
> **AP Style:**
> How could you? ...

9.11 | If a clause ends with an ellipsis and it is a complete sentence, and if the sentence would normally be terminated with a period, for Chicago Style, write four dots (the three ellipsis points followed by a full stop); or the period can be omitted. In AP Style, write the full stop, then a space, followed by the three points of the ellipsis. The variations shown below are all correct.

> **Closed Ellipsis:**
> ☺ Now you've really done it....
> ☺ Now you've really done it...
>
> **Open Ellipsis:**
> ☺ Now you've really done it . . . .
> ☺ Now you've really done it . . .
>
> **AP Style:**
> ☺ Now you've really done it. ...

9.12 | In a compound sentence connected by an ellipsis, you can sometimes omit the ending punctuation on the first clause, use only the ellipsis, and then end the compound sentence with the appropriate mark, such as a full stop or question mark.

Closed Ellipsis:
☺ What the heck...? Who ate the ice cream?
☺ What the heck...Who ate the ice cream?

Open Ellipsis:
☺ What the heck . . . ? Who ate the ice cream?
☺ What the heck . . . Who ate the ice cream?

AP Style:
☺ What the heck? ... Who ate the ice cream?
☺ What the heck ... Who ate the ice cream?

9.13 | If a phrase that is not a complete sentence ends with an ellipsis, write only the ellipsis; do not add a full stop.

Closed Ellipsis:
✗ What the....
☺ What the...

Open Ellipsis:
✗ What the....
☺ What the...

AP Style:
✗ What the ...
☺ What the ...

9.14 | If an ellipsis is used within a sentence, and the phrase before it requires a comma or some other punctuation mark, write the ellipsis after the mark, or ideally, omit the mark if you can do so without making the sentence ambiguous or confusing.

Closed Ellipsis:

Preferred: You can run...but you cannot hide.

Also Correct: You can run,...but you cannot hide.

Open Ellipsis:

Preferred: You can run . . . but you cannot hide.

Also Correct: You can run, . . . but you cannot hide.

AP Style:

Preferred: You can run ... but you cannot hide.

Also Correct: You can run, ... but you cannot hide.

9.15 | In writing dialogue, an ellipsis indicates speech trailing off. In these instances, do not use a period, comma, or semicolon after an ellipsis. Treat the ellipsis as a full stop.

Closed Ellipsis:

✗ "One day, aliens will land and...," William whispered.

☺ "One day, aliens will land and..." William whispered.

Open Ellipsis:

✗ "One day, aliens will land and . . . ," William whispered.

☺ "One day, aliens will land and . . ." William whispered.

AP Style:

✗ "One day, aliens will land and ... ," William whispered.

☺ "One day, aliens will land and ..." William whispered.

9.16 | Two or more ellipses may be used in a sentence, and the same rules apply to each of them.

Closed Ellipsis:

What I mean is...I just want to say...Oh, never mind.

Open Ellipsis:

What I mean is . . . I just want to say . . . Oh, never mind.

AP Style:

What I mean is ... I just want to say ... Oh, never mind.

9.17 | When text is quoted from a printed source (a book, newspaper, court transcript, etc.), or from an online source such as a website, use an ellipsis to indicate words omitted to save space or for brevity.

Closed Ellipsis:

Britain voted to leave the European Union...Electoral officials announced that the "Leave" campaign received 17.4 million votes, compared to 16.1 million backing the status quo...The result sent shock waves through global financial markets.

Open Ellipsis:

Britain voted to leave the European Union . . . Electoral officials announced that the "Leave" campaign received 17.4 million votes, compared to 16.1 million backing the status quo . . . The result sent shock waves through global financial markets.

AP Style:

Britain voted to leave the European Union ... Electoral officials announced that the "Leave" campaign received 17.4 million votes, compared to 16.1 million backing the status quo ... The result sent shock waves through global financial markets.

9.18 | When text is quoted as described in Rule 9.17, an ellipsis is usually not placed before the first word or after the last word of the passage unless the writer intends for the sentence to be incomplete.

Chapter 10

Parentheses & Brackets

> "I have a similar affection for the parenthesis (but I always take most of my parentheses out, so as not to call undue attention to the glaring fact that I cannot think in complete sentences..."
>
> Sarah Vowell
> Take the Cannoli

Parentheses allow you to introduce into a sentence a phrase that is not directly connected to the main statement but helps to make it clear. Normally used in pairs, parentheses tend to be ignored by contemporary writers in favor of the dash. But this punctuation mark has legitimate uses and should not be overlooked by those wanting to add variety and interest to their writing style.

Brackets, discussed later this chapter, are often confused with parentheses. They are normally written in pairs but serve different purposes and should not be used where parentheses are clearly indicated. The rules outlined below explain when and how to correctly use brackets as well as parentheses in your writing.

Rules for Using Parentheses

10.01 | To indicate that nonrestrictive information in a sentence is of only minor importance, use parentheses instead of commas or dashes. As with dashes, this is always a judgment call.

> The records (which arrived in damaged condition) require immediate attention.

10.02 | When the unity of a sentence is broken or a parenthetic phrase disrupts the flow of a sentence too much to be set off by commas, the words causing the break should be captured in parentheses.

> The red Ford SUV was speeding (I witnessed it personally) just minutes before it ran off the road.

10.03 | Use parentheses to enclose an explanatory word that is not part of a written statement if doing so helps to eliminate confusion or enhances the clarity of the sentence.

> This year (1914) saw the outbreak of a war that engulfed Europe.
>
> I subscribe to the Santa Barbara (CA) News-Press (but spell out News-Press of Santa Barbara, California)

10.04 | A phrase may be introduced into a sentence that is not essentially connected to the main statement but adds further detail to the sentence. This phrase should be enclosed in parentheses.

> Suspension was inevitable when the student (who was on academic probation) was caught cheating on his math exam.
>
> The result (see fig. 2) is most unexpected.
>
> China is the main buyer (by value) of oil exports from Iran (23 percent in 2016).
>
> The speaker (Mr. Ryan) gaveled the House of Representatives to order.

Note that the dash is sometimes used instead of the parenthesis in expressions which are not too remote in thought from the main idea of the sentence. Substituting dashes in place of the parenthesis in the first example above would not be improper.

10.05 | Overuse of parentheses is not desirable and can detract from the clarity and flow of your writing. Before introducing parenthetical phrases into your sentences, consider whether other less conspicuous constructions, such as using commas and semicolons, are possible. Writing that has the fewest explanatory and complicated clauses is almost always viewed as being of higher quality and preferred by readers.

10.06 | Use parentheses when you introduce an acronym.

> The collection contains hundreds of documents pertaining to the formation of the Tennessee Valley Authority (TVA).

10.07 | Use parentheses to capture *i.e.* and *e.g.* expressions.

> Several species (e.g., the bald eagle and the spotted owl) have been removed from the endangered list.

10.08 | Use parentheses to enclose a number inserted to confirm a written value that is spelled out. This is common practice in contracts, legal documents, and business correspondence.

> This job must be completed in sixty (60) days.

> Employees are entitled to three (3) weeks of paid vacation after one (1) year of full-time employment.

10.09 | When content in parentheses spans more than one paragraph, start each paragraph with an opening parenthesis, and write the closing parenthesis at the end of the last paragraph.

> (This is paragraph 1.

> (This is paragraph 2.

> (This is paragraph 3.)

10.10 | Parentheses are used in reports of speeches to set off the name of the person who is being referenced, and to indicate reactions on the part of the audience.

> The honorable gentleman who introduced this legislation (Mr. Smith) knows more about global terrorism law than anyone on this floor. (Applause.)

> "My position is one of intense opposition to this bill. (Applause.) My voice and my influence shall be employed to the utmost in securing its defeat. (Cheers.)"

10.11 | The Latin word *sic,* meaning *thus,* may be placed in parentheses after a word in a quoted passage to show that an error has been observed, and that *thus* it was in the original. It's like saying, yes, this word is spelled incorrectly—it's how the word was spelled in the original document.

> "The love of nature is widely seperated (sic) from the love of gain."

The word *separated* is misspelled in the example, and the error is noted by the parenthetical reference.

10.12 | Use square brackets to form parentheses within parentheses.

> The collection contains the papers from the terms of three former Secretaries of State (John Hay [1898–1905], Elihu Root [1905–9], and Robert Bacon [1909]).

10.13 | Parentheses can be used to enclose letters or numbers designating items in a series, either at the beginning of a paragraph or within a paragraph.

> The building materials will be delivered in this order: (1) lumber, (2) drywall, (3) insulation, and (4) nails, screws, and tape.

> You will observe that the kerosene lantern is (a) an antique, (b) works well, and (3) the glass globe is very clear for its age.

> Paragraph 4(C)(2)(a) will be found on page 9.

10.14 | Parentheses can be used, in pairs or singly, to enclose letters or numbers that mark division and classification in arguments or precise statements. These lists may be presented in several ways:

> (a)
>
> a)
>
> (1)
>
> 1)

10.15 | When a number is followed by a letter in parentheses, no space is used between the number and the opening paren. But if the letter is not in parentheses and the number is repeated with each letter, write the letter after the number with no space between.

> 15(a). Nails, bolts, and screws
>
> 15a. Nails, bolts, and screws

10.16 | If a sentence contains more than one parenthetical reference, place the period outside the closing parenthesis of the last reference.

> This species of tree (see fig. 6) is found growing in every county of Oregon (see fig. 1).

10.17 | Use parentheses to enclose remarks apparently made by the writer of the text. Use square brackets to enclose remarks made by the editor or reviewer of that text.

> The employer's policy on overtime will be amended on March 2, 2016. (I fact-checked this myself.)
>
> The employer's policy on overtime will be amended on March 2, 2016. (I fact-checked this myself.) [Joyce, this doesn't seem right; please verify.]

10.18 | When an abbreviation ends with a period and falls within parentheses at the end of a sentence, the style guide you are following will dictate how to handle the closing punctuation. In Chicago Style, you put a period after the abbreviation, and a second period after the closing paren to properly end the sentence.

> ✗ This happened two hundred years ago (1816 A.D.)
>
> ☺ This happened two hundred years ago (1816 A.D.).

10.19 | A parenthetic reference at the end of a sentence is placed before the period, unless it is a complete sentence in itself; in that case, it needs a full stop inside the parenthesis to end it. The main sentence also requires a period. So you will have a construction such as that in the third example below.

> During the summer, I like iced tea, sodas, and ice cream (sometimes frozen yogurt).
>
> This species of tree (see fig. 6) is found growing in every county of Oregon (see fig. 1).
>
> President Obama signed the Affordable Care Act into law in 2010. (He was elected in 2008.).

10.20 | A parenthetical reference that forms a complete sentence and falls within another sentence does not require a period; put a full stop at the end of the main sentence. But if the sentence in parentheses requires a question mark or exclamation mark, punctuate it accordingly, and put a full stop at the end of the main sentence.

> Thirty-five years after his death, Robert Frost (have you ever read his work?) remains America's favorite poet.
>
> Thirty-five years after his death, Robert Frost remains America's favorite poet. (We remember him at Kennedy's inauguration.)

10.21 | Do not use a comma or punctuation mark other than a full stop after a closing paren unless it would be required even without the parenthesis. When other punctuation is used, it should follow the closing paren.

> They sent us (as they had agreed to do) all the papers in the case.
>
> We expect John to bring his roommate home with him (he has been very anxious to do so); but we expect no one else.

Rules for Using Brackets

10.31 | Use brackets to enclose words or phrases that are entirely independent of the rest of the sentence. The enclosed words are usually comments, queries, corrections, criticisms, or directions inserted by some person other than the original writer or speaker, often the editor or reviewer of a text (see Rule 10.17).

10.32 | Make sure you always use brackets in pairs; otherwise, readers may be easily confused about where the inserted material is supposed to begin or end. Follow this principle if you are putting heading numbers in brackets; always write [1] and not a single bracket, as 1]. But see Rule 10.40 for one important exception.

10.33 | Use brackets to enclose some statement or word of the writer that is thrown into a quotation by way of explanation or otherwise.

> His letter reads: "We have decided to ask Mr. Howard [his cousin] to deliver the address…"

10.34 | Use brackets to avoid the confusion that would otherwise be caused by a parenthesis nested within a parenthesis.

> On hot summer days, I like iced tea, lemonade, and ice cream (sometimes frozen [or refrigerated] yogurt).

10.35 | Brackets are used in bills, contracts, laws, etc., to indicate matter that is to be omitted.

10.36 | Brackets are used in various ways in mathematics.

> $[5 + 4 \times (5 + 6)]/7$
>
> $[10,6] = \text{LCM}(10,6) = 30$

10.37 | Brackets are used to enclose passages of doubtful authenticity in reprints of early manuscripts, amendments to legislative bills, legal documents, and other portions of a text that should be flagged as questionable.

10.38 | Brackets are used in legal and ecclesiastical papers to indicate numerical words that may have to be changed, or to indicate where details are to be supplied.

> This is the first [second or third] publication.
>
> The board members shall remain in office until [state date] or until their successors are trained and fully qualified.

10.39 | Brackets are used in court transcripts, government hearings, some legal documents, and other records to enclose interpolations that are not part of the original quotation, such as a correction, explanation, omission, editorial comment, or a notation that a particular error is reproduced literally.

> Our conference [lasted] two hours.
>
> The statue [sic] was on the law books.
>
> The general [MacArthur] ordered him to leave.
>
> The paper was as follows [reads]:
>
> I do not know. [Continues reading:]
>
> They fooled only themselves. [Laughter]
>
> The Witness: He did it that way [indicating].
>
> Q. Do you know these men? [Hands a list to the witness]
>
> Witness: This matter is classified. [Deleted]
>
> Mr. Jones: Please hold up your hands. [Show of hands]
>
> [Discussion off the record]
>
> Mr. Jones [continuing]: Now let us take the next item.
>
> Mr. Smith [presiding]: Do you mean that literally?
>
> The Chairman [to Mr. Smith]:
>
> [Mr. Smith makes a further statement off the record.]
>
> Speak up. [A voice from the audience]
>
> Be quiet! [Several voices from the audience]

10.40 | When content in brackets spans more than one paragraph, start each paragraph with a bracket, and write the closing bracket at the end of the last paragraph.

> [This is Paragraph 1.
>
> [This is Paragraph 2.
>
> [This is Paragraph 3.]

Notice the closing bracket at the end of the third paragraph.

Chapter 11

Quotation Marks

> "Have you ever observed that we pay much more attention to a wise passage when it is quoted, than when we read it in the original author?"
>
> Philip Gilbert Hamerton
> The Intellectual Life

Quotation marks are used to set off the exact words spoken or written by someone else. Also called quote marks, and inverted commas, this symbol was developed by French printers in the 1500s. At first, only a single quotation mark was used, and it was placed in the outside margin of a page to call attention to an important passage, not just a quotation. By the mid-sixteenth century, its appearance had changed to the double inverted comma that we use today. In the seventeenth century, printers began utilizing this mark in pairs to set off quotations. The single quotation mark was introduced in the early 1800s as a way to mark a nested quote within a quote.

In addition to setting off direct quotations, this punctuation mark has a few other uses in modern writing, as described in these next pages.

11.01 | Use quotation marks to indicate the beginning and end of words borrowed from another person or source. A comma usually precedes the quotation if you include it in your own sentence. But if the quotation is just a few words, see Rule 11.02; and when the quotation is longer, or it is introduced in a formal manner, use a colon instead, as in the third and fourth examples below.

The Senator said, "We must hurry and pass the bill within thirty days."

Bob shouted, "Run! That man has a gun!"

The textbook stated: "Scientists use the scientific method to answer questions about the natural world around us. It is a series of steps that help to investigate a question."

Responding to the question, the economist replied: "The stock market is unpredictable, driven by world events beyond the control of most investors. There is no guarantee that a stock investment will be profitable."

11.02 | Do not use a comma before or after a quotation when it is a short phrase or fragment integrated into the sentence.

✘ According to the mayor, crime in Chicago, "increased significantly" last year.

☺ According to the mayor, crime in Chicago "increased significantly" last year.

11.03 | If a quotation forms a complete sentence, it must have an ending punctuation mark. Often, this will be a full stop, or a comma followed by the conclusion of your own sentence, and it should be placed inside the closing quotation mark (in American English; outside the closing quote mark in British English). The following examples show sentences with quotations marked in a variety of ways.

Bob asked, "How are you doing today?"

Mary scowled and said, "I have a headache."

"Oh no!" Bob exclaimed.

"I'll take an aspirin," Mary replied.

"You take too much aspirin. I worry that…"

Mary snapped, "Bob, stop! You worry too much."

11.04 | Reports of what another person said or wrote in words other than his own are called **indirect quotations**. Do not use quotation marks on these statements.

> The accountant said that his client had run out of money.
>
> According to the textbook, studies in the early twentieth century revealed a relationship between light and an atom's electrons.
>
> He said he would go to the party if he could.
>
> But: He said, "I would go if I could."

11.05 | At the end of a quotation in your own sentence, add the punctuation mark that you need for your sentence. If your sentence ends with a quotation, then put a full stop or other appropriate point inside the closing quote mark. If your sentence continues on, then provide a comma inside the closing quote mark and a terminating mark at the end of your sentence. If necessary, remove the last punctuation mark in the original quotation to avoid a double punctuation mark, one from the borrowed text and one for your own sentence. Notice the following:

> ✗ I like the remark "Give me liberty, or give me death.", but I think it's a dangerous principle.

Since your sentence continues beyond the end of the quotation, remove the full stop at the end of the quotation, even though that is what occurs in the original text. Your sentence requires a comma.

> ☺ I like the remark "Give me liberty, or give me death," but I think it's a dangerous principle.

But if the quotation ends with a question mark or an exclamation point, retain it, whether or not your sentence comes to an end. If your sentence does end at the conclusion of the quotation, do not add a second punctuation mark to terminate your sentence. Notice these examples:

> When she called out "Who's there?" I did not answer.

> The opening line of Hamlet is "Who's there?" The line is significant.
>
> Archimedes cried out "Eureka!" when he had solved the problem.

11.06 | Inside the quotation marks, replicate exactly the punctuation, capitalization, and language of the original text. Do not change anything, except at the very end as required to follow these rules.

11.07 | Place a question mark inside the closing quotation mark if the quotation is a question, but outside if the quotation is not a question yet the entire sentence is. Notice the following examples:

> She asked me, "Why didn't you call?"
>
> [The question mark is inside the quotation because the quotation is a question, but the total sentence is not.]
>
> Did Shakespeare write the passage, "What's in a name?"
>
> [Here the entire sentence is a question, and so is the quotation. The question mark (part of the original text) stays inside the quotation marks, and no additional question mark is used to show that the entire sentence is a question.]
>
> What do you mean when you say that you are "so over it all"?
>
> [Here the question mark is outside the closing quotation mark because the entire sentence is a question, but the quotation is not.]

11.08 | Semicolons and colons always go outside the closing quotation mark.

> Shakespeare did not write, "To err is human; to forgive divine"; Alexander Pope did.

11.09 | When several words or very short phrases in a series are quoted individually, enclose each within its own pair of quotation marks, and put a comma inside the closing quotation mark at the end of each. Follow the rule about using serial commas (discussed in an earlier chapter), if your style guide recommends them.

✗ In this passage, the words "shining" "cold" "vibrant" and "glittering" have special importance.

☺ In this passage, the words "shining," "cold," "vibrant," and "glittering" have special importance.

11.10 | Use single quotation marks to set off quoted passages within double quotation marks. If within these internally quoted words another quotation is introduced, this is surrounded by the double points.

> Her supervisor explained, "The benefits handbook says 'employees shall be entitled to two weeks of annual vacation leave,' not three weeks."

Limit alternations between double and single quotes to three sets (double, single, double). If a sentence contains more than three sets of quotation marks, rewrite it to avoid this awkward construction.

> The policeman said: "We received a tip from an anonymous caller who claimed, 'A man dressed in military fatigues yelled, "Die, you scum!" and then he detonated a bomb and blew up the restaurant.'"

11.11 | When the single and double quotation marks both come at the end of quotation, include them both, as in the above example and in the following:

> "Emily told me, 'I loathe figs.'"

11.12 | Do not use single quotation marks where double quotation marks are customary. Confine your use of single quotation marks to those rare occasions when you have to indicate a quotation within a quotation.

11.13 | If you interrupt a quotation to indicate a speaker, then you must use the appropriate punctuation. In the following example, the interruption is treated as a parenthetic insertion, set off with a pair of commas. The quotation is, in effect, a single sentence with an interruption in the middle.

> "The fact that *war* is the word we use for almost everything," writes journalist Glenn Greenwald, "has certainly helped to desensitize us to its invocation; if we wage wars on drugs, terror, poverty, and everything else, how bad can they be?"

In this next example, a comma separates the first sentence of the quotation from the interruption. But after the interruption there is a full stop because the quotation continues, beginning a new sentence.

> "Our city has become a dangerous place," said the police chief. "We must restore law and order."

11.14 | When you wish to omit text from the middle of a sentence in a quotation because the material is irrelevant to the point you are making, use an ellipsis in place of the text.

> "The building codes specify electrical wiring standards…and plumbing regulations."

11.15 | If you wish to omit some words that come at the end of a sentence in the original quotation, or if you wish to omit a complete sentence from the quotation, use four dots: a full stop, followed by an ellipsis (three spaced dots); or, if your style guide advises against spaces, type four periods with no spaces.

> In this connection, Brunke commented, "The death of Alexander the Great raises difficulties for the historian. . . . The evidence is unreliable and contradictory. . . ."

In this example, the four dots in the middle of the quotation indicate that the writer has omitted some words from the end of the sentence or an intervening sentence in the original text. The four dots at the end indicate that the quotation ends before the sentence in the original does. Note the spacing of these dots: none between the last word in the sentence and the first period, and a single space between each of the three dots of the ellipsis.

11.16 | Use ellipsis marks intelligently when you want to omit from a quotation something you don't need to make your point. Do not use them as convenient shorthand to save yourself the trouble of writing out the quotation in full. What you omit from the quotation should be irrelevant to your purpose in introducing the quotation.

11.17 | Do not use ellipsis marks to indicate very large omissions. If you are quoting two or more parts significantly separated from each other in the original, then offer them as two or more separate quotations. Do not, for example, write something like the following:

> ✗ Very significant in this respect are the following phrases "vegetation rioted ... mob of island ... lost your way."

Since these phrases occur in separate sentences and quite far apart in the original, offer them as three separate short quotations:

> ☺ Very significant in this respect are the following phrases: "vegetation rioted," "mob of islands," and "lost your way."

Note carefully the punctuation of this list of short quotations, especially the relationship between the commas and the closing quotation marks. This follows Rule 11.09.

11.18 | In quotations, ellipses may be combined with other punctuation, such as a comma, a period, or a question mark. Do not include a space between the final ellipsis point and the punctuation.

> "Will you come...?"

11.19 | Check the accuracy of all quotations carefully. Do not misquote. The words and punctuation must appear exactly as they do in the original text (but see Rule 11.06 about ending punctuation). Never add more information to a quotation, even in parenthesis (but see Rule 11.20). This restriction includes adding definitions, clarifications, or correcting factual errors. Put the new information in a footnote or in a separate sentence following the quotation.

11.20 | If you wish to put a comment of your own into the middle of a quotation, use square brackets. Normally you will do this only to clarify a pronoun or to remind the reader that a mistake in the quotation belongs to the original and is not a misprint of your own.

> Stein writes, "[Homer] is incredibly [sic] long winded."

Stein originally wrote "he," but you want the reader to understand who is being discussed, so you put Homer's name into the quotation; the square brackets indicate the change. The [sic] indicates to the reader that the misspelling of "incredibly" is in the original text, not your mistake.

11.21 | Do not use the square brackets to change quotations unnecessarily, for example, by changing the verbs or the pronouns. Leave the original unchanged, except for the rare cases mentioned in the preceding rule.

11.22 | Make sure that the quotations you offer make sense. In other words, write out enough of the original material so that the meaning of your sentence is clear and complete. Be particularly careful when you are setting up a quotation as an example.

> ✗ Sally evidently is a good housekeeper. For example, the first descriptions of the house "the kitchen clean as a whistle ... and the polished floor."

Here the second sentence is a fragment. You will have to change it so as to avoid the fragment.

11.23 | Double quotation marks are used sometimes to draw attention to an unusual or non-standard word or phrase. This practice is not very common in formal writing and should be avoided entirely in technical writing. Rather than using quote marks, it is better to write words and phrases that you wish to emphasize in italics.

> ✗ The oil extraction process is called "fracking."
> ☺ The oil extraction process is called *fracking*.

Sometimes, though, the writer may wish to call attention to specific words that a person actually has spoken. The following sentence could be written without the quotation marks, but using them calls attention to the fact that the words were spoken and not merely the writer's own verbiage to make a point.

> The ill-tempered man often calls the school children who walk in front of his house "idiots" and "delinquents," and he shouts obscenities at them. One young girl yelled back today and called the man "a mean old creep."

Similarly, in a passage quoted in the indirect form, if only part of the sentence is an exact quote, it should be placed in quotation marks.

> The governor applauded the legislators' action and declared that his state "would not tolerate unsafe conditions" in nursing homes, adding that "safety violations will be prosecuted to the full extent of the law."

11.24 | If you decide to emphasize part of a quotation by putting that section in italics or a bold font, then you must indicate to the reader that you have changed the original. The normal way to accomplish this is to write immediately after the quotation the parenthetical comment "emphasis added" in brackets, as in the following example:

> The report published by the government stressed that "*this part of the coast should never again be an active logging site.*"[emphasis added]

11.25 | If a quotation consists of several paragraphs, place an opening quotation mark in front of each paragraph, and end the last paragraph with a closing quotation mark.

> "The first paragraph...no closing quote mark.
>
> "The second paragraph...no closing quote mark.
>
> "The third paragraph...note the closing quotation mark."

11.26 | Use quotation marks or italics to enclose any matter following such terms as *the word, the term, named, entitled, cited as, referred* *to as,* or *signed.* Chicago Style prefers italics be used for this purpose, but quotation marks are acceptable at the writer's discretion. As always when we discuss style, consistency throughout the entirety of the manuscript or document is important, and you should choose one method or the other and stick with.

☺ The letter was signed *John Quincy Smith.*

☺ The letter was signed "John Quincy Smith."

☺ Be sure to spell the word *caricature* correctly.

☺ Be sure to spell the word "caricature" correctly.

Do not use quotation marks or italics to set off expressions that follow the terms *known as, called, so-called,* and so forth, unless such expressions are misnomers or slang.

☺ The man known as The Zodiac Killer was never caught.

☺ He didn't like any of the so-called candidates.

11.27 | When information is enclosed within quotation marks, and the reader must understand that ending punctuation or other marks are not part of the quoted matter, the point should be placed outside the closing quote mark. For example, in a tutorial on using Microsoft Windows, you might need to instruct the reader to type a specific command; placing the terminating full stop at the end of the sentence outside of the closing quotation mark makes it clear that the full stop itself should not be typed.

✗ Open a command prompt and type "regedit."

☺ Open a command prompt and type "regedit".

In the first example above, it's not clear to the reader whether the ending period should be typed as part of the command. Placing the full stop outside of the closing quotation mark, as in the second example, clearly shows that it is not part of the instruction.

Here are two more examples:

> On page 10 of your draft, at the end of the first sentence, type the word "maintenance".
>
> Change "February 1, 2016" to "May 30, 2016".

11.28 | Use quotation marks to set off misnomers, slang expressions, coined words, and words or phrases used in a notable, ironic, or unusual manner.

> It was a "gentlemen's agreement."
>
> The "invisible government" is responsible.
>
> Her "beautiful smile" is as fake as a three-dollar bill.
>
> George Herman "Babe" Ruth.
>
> After the word "treaty," insert a comma.
>
> The check was endorsed "John Adamson."

11.29 | Sentences from a foreign language are usually enclosed in quotation marks. Single foreign words should be written in italics. But if a foreign word is widely used and the writer believes it is familiar to most readers, it need not be italicized.

11.30 | Avoid overuse of quotation marks. Familiar expressions, clichés, and sayings most readers have heard numerous times before need not be quoted. Lists of words presented merely as words, and lists of books, plays, movies, or songs, should be printed without quotation marks. Excessive use of quote marks can spoil the look of the page and make the content difficult to read.

11.31 | When quoting a passage of poetry or prose longer than three lines, set it in its own block, indent the left margin, and do not use quotation marks. If you are double spacing your document, also double space the quotation.

11.32 | Make sure your own sentence comes to a natural ending before you start a long quotation in its own block. Thus, after the quotation you should be starting a new sentence in your own paragraph. Do not break a sentence of your own with a long quotation.

11.33 | Quotation marks are not used in poetry, except to set off dialogue spoken in the poem.

11.34 | When you quote a short passage of prose or poetry (three lines or less), use double quotation marks, and set the quotation within your own paragraph.

> Alice Baird, reflecting on this point, makes the following observation: "In retrospect, Alexander the Great's dream for a cultural and political union of east and west seems hopelessly ambitious." This view is worth exploring.

11.35 | When you quote a short selection of poetry (three lines or less) in your own sentence, indicate the line endings with a solidus or slash (/). Leave a space after the solidus.

> My favorite limerick begins as follows: "An Italian who loved fettucini/ Fed tons to his hungry bambini./ But they knew the score. . . ." I cannot remember the rest.

11.36 | With more than three lines of poetry, set the quotation in a separate block, without quotation marks, following as closely as possible the format of the original text (including the spelling, the arrangement of lines, and the punctuation). Indent the poem on the left, and double space the quotation.

11.37 | When you set a selection of poetry in its own paragraph, do not use the solidus or slash (/) to indicate the line endings. They will be clear from the format of the quotation.

11.38 | Do not use the solidus to indicate line endings in prose quotations, either for quotations in your sentence or in their own blocks. In prose quotations set in their own blocks, you do not have to follow the original layout of the text from which you are taking the material. But the prose quotation must be indented in the usual way, and observe the same right-hand margin as the main text of the paper.

11.39 | If you are quoting a selection of verse in its own block and wish to leave out a few lines, then indicate the omission with a row of spaced full stops across the length of the line, as follows:

> If music be the food of love, play on,
>
> Give me excess of it, that, surfeiting,
>
> The appetite may sicken, and so die.
>
> That strain again! It had a dying fall;
>
> . . . .
>
> So full of shapes is fancy
>
> That it alone is high fantastical.

Normally, you should use this technique only if the omission is quite short. If you wish to leave out a substantial amount (more than a couple of lines), then present the two sections as two separate quotations with a space between them.

Chapter 12

Apostrophes

> "The apostrophe must be the most misunderstood and misused piece of punctuation in the language. This is made worse by the fact that most people simply fail to understand what it does."
>
> Patrick Notchtree
> "Apostrophe Catastrophe"

The apostrophe, which has the appearance of a closing single quotation mark, has various uses in the English language. It can form the possessive case for singular and plural nouns, noun phrases, and pronouns (the man's book, Robert's wife, the cars' buyers). It can indicate omitted letters, as with contractions (don't, can't, wouldn't); and it can form certain plural nouns, such as single letters and digits (I count three 4's and six b's on that page; Be sure to dot your i's). This mark has other uses as well, which are detailed in this chapter.

The first known use of the apostrophe dates back to the late 1400s in France. It soon found its way into English literature, where it stood for a missing letter or a contraction. By the eighteenth century, rules for writing possessives and plurals were widely observed in Europe.

Some writers dismiss apostrophes as elementary and easy to figure out. But this mark is more versatile than meets the eye, and to master it, you need to learn more than two dozen rules and exceptions. Some of these rules are fairly complex and at the root of frequent confusion and writing errors. In some cases, a misplaced or incorrectly used apostrophe can change the meaning of a sentence to something other than what the writer intended.

The rules for possessive apostrophes, and plural possessives in particular, confuse many writers. The fact that these rules vary from one style guide to another complicates matters. The guidelines and examples in this chapter rely on Chicago Style unless otherwise noted. If you are using another style guide, consult the applicable sections for the rules on handling apostrophes.

12.01 | Form the possessive case for singular and plural common nouns that do not end with *s* by adding an apostrophe and an *s*.

Singular nouns:

a woman's hat

his dog's collar

the teacher's lecture

the plumber's tools

Plural nouns:

gentlemen's agreement

people's choice

the children's toys

the women's purses

12.02 | Form the possessive case for singular common nouns that end with *s* by adding an apostrophe and an *s*.

My boss's watch was stolen.

The witness's testimony was not credible.

The bus's tire went flat on the mountain road.

12.03 | Form the possessive case for proper nouns ending in *s*, where the *s* is pronounced, by adding an apostrophe and an *s* if singular; or if plural, as in the third example below, use only an apostrophe.

Bernie Sanders's campaign
[Mr. Sanders is one person, so add apostrophe + s]

Bill Gates's foundation
[Mr. Gates is one person, so add apostrophe + s]

the Obamas' family portrait
[*The Obamas* refers to multiple people in Obama's family, so simply add an apostrophe at the end of the name]

Some writers add an apostrophe and omit the possessive *s* after common nouns that end in *s* (for example, Bernie Sanders' speech). If you adhere to Chicago Style, this practice is considered antiquated, and the above rule should be followed.

12.04 | For common nouns and proper nouns ending in an unpronounced *s*, form the possessive case by adding an apostrophe + *s*.

> Descartes's writings are the foundation of Western philosophy.
>
> Arkansas's northern border is Missouri's southern border.

12.05 | For singular common nouns that end in *s* and are followed by a word that begins with an *s*, add an apostrophe to form the possessive case.

> For goodness' sake, please stop!
>
> for old times' sake

12.06 | For singular common nouns that end with an *s* sound but not the letter *s*, add an apostrophe and an *s* to form the possessive case.

> Science's 2015 breakthrough was a genome-editing technique.
>
> For appearance's sake, wear a shirt and tie.
>
> She should tell her husband for her conscience's sake.

Rewriting a sentence may be the best way to avoid clumsy syntax and improve the flow. Recasting the three sentences above, as we can see below, would eliminate the awkward use of possessive apostrophes.

> The science breakthrough of 2015 was a genome-editing technique.
>
> For the sake of appearance, wear a shirt and tie.
>
> She should tell her husband for the sake of her conscience.

12.07 | For plural common nouns ending in *s*, form the possessive case by adding an apostrophe.

> the politicians' committee
>
> the students' books
>
> the four dogs' collars
>
> The three moms' kids were well-behaved.

12.08 | For nouns plural in form (ending in *s*) but that have singular meaning, add an apostrophe to form the possessive case.

> the Westworld series' actors
>
> Measles' symptoms can be quite painful.
>
> the Asian countries' trade agreement

12.09 | For compound nouns, form the possessive case by adding an apostrophe + *s* to the element nearest the object possessed.

> The saw blade's edge was quite dull.
>
> The reaction to the attorney general's decision was swift.

12.10 | Joint possession is indicated by placing an apostrophe on the last element of a series. By contrast, individual or alternative possession requires the use of an apostrophe on each element in the series.

> David and Karen's racy novel raised eyebrows.
>
> [David and Karen are writing a novel together, so use one apostrophe on the last element.]

David's and Karen's novels may become bestsellers.

[David and Karen are writing separate novels, so both names require an apostrophe to show individual possession.]

12.11 | Do not use an apostrophe after the names of countries or organized bodies ending in the letter *s*. Otherwise, use an apostrophe and add *s*.

> Russia's oil exports
>
> House of Representatives session
>
> United States influence
>
> United Nations diplomats
>
> Massachusetts laws

12.12 | Possessive pronouns do not take an apostrophe—only nouns can have a possessive case that requires an apostrophe. The possessive pronouns are: *hers, his, ours, yours, theirs,* and *its.*

Remember: *its* is a possessive pronoun; *it's* is an abbreviation for it is.

12.13 | Don't use an apostrophe after words more descriptive than possessive (does not indicate personal possession), except when a plural does not end in *s*.

> **Nouns more descriptive than possessive:**
>
> > Writers Workshop
> >
> > Proofreaders Guidelines
>
> **Nouns more descriptive than possessive but don't end in *s*:**
>
> > women's fashion
> >
> > children's hospital
> >
> > men's restroom

12.14 | Possessive indefinite and impersonal pronouns require an apostrophe.

The authors autographed each other's books.

That was another's idea.

They dressed in some others' clothing.

Why is someone's footprint outside my window?

It is said that one's eyes are a reflection of the soul.

12.15 | Use an apostrophe to indicate omission of letters in dialect, in contractions, and in poetry.

I'm = I am

who's = who is

didn't = did not

could've = could have

That's 'ow 'tis = That's how it is

'Twas so easy = It was so easy

aren't = are not

d'you = do you

should've = should have [*not* should of!]

12.16 | The singular possessive case is used in general terms such as the following:

arm's length	attorney's fees
baker's dozen	editor's revisions
printer's ink	confectioner's sugar
buyer's remorse	cow's milk
writer's cramp	doctor's advice

12.17 | Four-digit year dates can be abbreviated by substituting an apostrophe for the first two digits, although the practice is frowned upon because it creates ambiguity.

The Spirit of '76

The summer of '65

The Art Deco era was in the '20s.

12.18 | Use the apostrophe to form the plural of letters and digits.

This sentence contains six lower case e's and no 2's.

Cross your t's and dot your i's.

Computers run binary code made up of a series of 0's and 1's.

12.19 | While an apostrophe is used to indicate possession and contractions, it is not necessary to use an apostrophe to show the plural form of most initials, acronyms, and abbreviations, except where required to enhance clarity or eliminate confusion.

ABCs

1920s

49ers

FAQs

during the twenties

2-by-4s (or two-by-fours)

IOUs, IPOs, SUVs

in her 70s (better: in her seventies)

during the '20s (better: during the 1920s)

Watch your p's and q's.

12.20 | When an acronym is shown in parenthesis, add a lower case *s* within the parentheses to show its plural form.

(SUVs), (JPEGs), (IPOs), (MP3s)

12.21 | Omit the apostrophe in the shortened forms of most commonly used words.

Halloween, not Hallowe'en

possum, not 'possum

But ma'am requires an apostrophe, and so does o'clock.

12.22 | The plural of spelled-out numbers is formed by adding *s* or *es*, as in the following.

fives, sixes, and sevens

12.23 | The plural of words referred to as words, and words containing an apostrophe, is formed by adding *s* or *es*. But an apostrophe and an *s* is added to indicate the plural of words used as words if omitting the apostrophe would make the passage difficult to read.

yeas and nays

ins and outs

the haves and have-nots

yeses and noes

ands, ifs, and buts

ups and downs

do's and don'ts

12.24 | The possessive case is often used in lieu of an objective phrase, even though direct ownership is not involved.

for charity's sake

a stone's throw

one dollar's worth

five dollars' worth [but $200 million worth]

one day's labor

four weeks' pay

12 days' labor

12.25 | A possessive noun used in an adjective sense requires the addition of an apostrophe + *s*.

She is a friend of Lisa's.

Kevin's is the white house on the corner.

12.26 | A noun that precedes a gerund should be written in the possessive case. A **gerund** is a word derived from a verb but that serves as a noun and ends in *-ing*. In the two examples below, the gerunds are italicized; the possessive nouns are italicized and underlined.

We expected <u>*Alice's*</u> *meddling*, so no one was surprised.

<u>*Jason's*</u> *whining* irritated everyone at the party.

Chapter 13

Other Symbols

> "Let grammar, punctuation, and spelling into your life! Even the most energetic and wonderful mess has to be turned into sentences."
>
> Terry Pratchett

& Ampersand

13.01 | The ampersand is used interchangeably with the word "and." Most style guides advise against writing this symbol in running copy, headings, or titles, except in limited situations. Thus, you should write *black and white* rather than *black & white*, *imports and exports* rather than *imports & exports*.

13.02 | Some companies use the ampersand in their official names. When it is part of a company's legal name, write the symbol; do not substitute the word *and* in its place. The companies in the following three examples all use the ampersand in their legal names, so these examples are written correctly.

☺ Dun & Bradstreet

☺ Tiffany & Co.

☺ JP Morgan Chase & Co.

13.03 | In an abbreviated company name that is commonly used in place of the full name (as *AT&T Corp.*, short for *American Telephone and Telegraph*), and where the abbreviation includes an ampersand, write the symbol and do not substitute the word *and* in its place.

✗ AT and T

☺ AT&T

13.04 | The same rule applies when an ampersand is used in the title of a book, song, report, or other work. Do not substitute an ampersand if the word *and* appears in the title. In the examples below, the word *and* is used properly in each title, so replacing it with an ampersand would be incorrect.

> ✗ Romeo & Juliet, Two & a Half Men, Harry Potter & the Philosopher's Stone

> ☺ Romeo and Juliet, Two and a Half Men, Harry Potter and the Philosopher's Stone

13.05 | The ampersand is sometimes used within tables and parentheses when space is limited.

13.06 | Use the ampersand when it appears in common expressions where readers typically expect to see the symbol rather than the word *and* spelled out.

> ☺ rock & roll (or rock 'n roll)

> ☺ country & western

> ☺ R&R (common abbreviation for "rest and recuperation")

13.07 | In citations when a source has more than one author, APA and some other style guides advise that the last two should be connected by an ampersand (*Bailey, Cohen & Winters, 2015*); Chicago Style and MLA recommend that *and* be spelled out. APA likewise accepts the use of the ampersand to link author names in in-text citations (*Clark & Adams, 1998*), while others recommend writing out the word.

13.08 | The term *et cetera*, which means "and so forth," is commonly abbreviated as *etc.* and occasionally written as *&c.* This practice was more prevalent in literature of the early twentieth century. Many readers today are not familiar with this form, so its use should be avoided to prevent confusion.

* (Asterisk)

13.10 | The asterisk, derived from a Greek word that means "little star," has a number of uses. One of the most common is to indicate a footnote, or to refer to an annotation of special terms or conditions. When it is utilized as a footnote in text, always write the symbol and never spell out the word "asterisk."

13.11 | The asterisk is sometimes used as a low-tech substitute for a bullet that precedes an item in a list.

> * bread
>
> * milk
>
> * eggs

13.12 | The asterisk is commonly used in email messages, social network chat, texting, and other similar applications to emphasize a word or phrase when other enhancements, such as bold and italic font styles, are not available to the writer. Note that the underscore often is used in the same manner.

> ☺ Do *not* talk to me about politics or religion!
>
> ☺ Charles is grouchy and _really_ needs a vacation!

13.13 | The asterisk can be substituted in place of one or more letters in an expletive ("Oh s**t!") so that the writer does not have to spell out a word some readers may find offensive.

13.14 | Asterisks may be substituted for letters in a person's name to mask the individual's identity.

> The witness, J****, initially was afraid to testify.

13.15 | In arithmetic, the asterisk is commonly used as the symbol of multiplication.

> 3 * 6 = 18

13.16 | In computer science, the asterisk is used as a "wildcard" character. For instance, when deleting files from a hard drive, if you specify a pattern that includes a wildcard, such as *sa*.txt*, all files with names that begin with the letters "sa" and end with ".txt" would be deleted.

13.17 | In some computer programming languages (C, PHP, Java, Javascript, and others), a pair of asterisks and matching forward slashes can be used to embed a comment within program code. Setting off a comment in this manner identifies it as a notation and prevents the program from trying to execute it as part of the code.

/* This is a comment */

@ (At Sign)

13.20 | The "at sign" may be utilized in a variety of ways too numerous to fully list here, but one common practice is using the symbol to specify unit pricing, as in *bread, 2 loaves @ 1.00 each*.

13.21 | In computing, the @ symbol is used in every valid email address, setting off the names of users from their email domains (*bill.smith@gmail.com; president@whitehouse.gov*).

13.22 | On some social networks, the @ symbol is placed before a name or nickname to identify a particular user. For instance, you can follow *@jedi_editor* (the author/editor of this book) on Twitter. On Facebook, typing a valid username preceded by the "@" symbol while composing a message will result in that user's full name being inserted into the post, replacing the @ symbol and the username.

° (Degree Sign)

13.30 | The degree sign is a typographic symbol commonly used to express temperatures and angles. For example, the normal human body temperature is 98.6° Fahrenheit, and a square has four 90° angles. The symbol often appears in scientific and technical literature, but most style guides recommend that writers spell out the word *degrees* when writing for a general audience. But in scientific writing, the symbol is generally preferred and should be used unless writers are expected to follow a style guide that recommends otherwise.

☺ A square has four 90-degree angles.

☺ Water boils at 212 degrees Fahrenheit.

" (Ditto Mark)

13.35 | The ditto mark is a typographic symbol that means the words, numbers, or other data above it are to be repeated.

```
100 watt lightbulbs, $3.99 each
 75     "           "      $2.99  "
```

¢ (Cent Sign)

13.40 | The cent symbol derives from the Latin word *centum*, which means "hundred." It denotes a penny in US currency, and one hundred pennies add up to a dollar. The symbol is used in other monetary systems as well. It is used in advertising brochures occasionally to indicate the price of an item (*tomatoes on sale, 50¢ a pound*) but rarely in formal writing. Most style guides recommend that references to cents should be spelled out.

> My favorite candy bar used to cost five cents. Today, it costs almost one dollar.

$ (Dollar Sign)

13.45 | Speaking of dollars, this instantly recognizable symbol that many people associate with the US dollar was first used to denote the Mexican peso. It is associated with other global currencies as well. Some style guides advise that *dollars* should be spelled out rather than using the symbol; but books, magazines, and websites devoted to business, finance, investing, and the like frequently use the dollar sign in news stories and other content. If a global audience is served, the abbreviation *US* should precede the dollar sign when it refers to American dollars; for example, *US$5 million* or *US $5 million*. The space between "US" and the symbol is optional.

13.46 | In computer science, the dollar sign is used in some programming languages to identify string variables and for other purposes. The symbol often appears in books, articles, and other content related to computers and programming. When used in these contexts, always write the symbol and never spell out the word *dollar*.

(Hash, Pound, or Number Sign)

13.50 | The hash, pound, or number symbol occasionally is written as shorthand for the word "pounds" (*5# apples* means five pounds of apples). Likewise, the symbol can be placed in front of a digit to designate a number ranking, such as *#1 Bestseller.*

13.51 | The hash symbol is used in a variety of ways in computer programming languages and by operating systems. When placed on the first line of an executable script and immediately followed by an exclamation point (#!), it is often called a *shebang* and tells the operating system which program should be used to run the script, as well as where that program is located on the hard drive or server. In some languages, it can be used to set off a non-executing comment placed in the program code.

> # This is a comment

The hash symbol can signify certain types of program variables and arrays, channel names on an IRC chat server, and it has numerous other uses. When used in these contexts, write the # symbol rather than spelling out "hash symbol" or a similar term (but see Rule 14.51 for an exception).

13.52 | On social media sites, especially Twitter, the term *hashtag* refers to the practice of placing a hash symbol before a keyword to associate a message containing that keyword with a particular topic. For instance, the most popular hashtags on Twitter in 2016 were *#Rio2016*, *#Election2016*, *#PokemonGo*, *#Euro2016*, and *#Oscars*. Notice that the keyword follows the hash, and no spaces appear in the hashtag.

% (Percent)

13.60 | The percent symbol is often found in modern writing, but most style guides have firm rules about how and when it should be used, and whether the word *percent* should be substituted in place of it. Some handbooks favor the use of the symbol when a number is expressed (50%), while others recommend the spelled-out form (*50* *percent*). Chicago Style breaks content into two categories: humanist, for a general audience, and scientific/statistical. When writing for the former, use digits and spell the word *percent*; for the latter audience, use digits followed by the percent sign.

Humanistic:
He won the election with 51 percent of the vote.

Scientific/statistical:
In the clinical trial, 17% of the patients reported adverse reactions to the experimental drug.

13.61 | Never write the percent sign after a spelled-out number.

✗ The pollster estimated only thirty% of the state's Democrats voted in the election.

☺ The pollster estimated only 30 percent of the state's Democrats voted in the election.

13.62 | Never begin a sentence with a digit. Write the number as a word if it begins the sentence; or if the resulting construction is awkward, recast the sentence. In the following example, since we cannot begin the sentence with "17%," the only workaround is to rewrite it.

✗ 17% of the patients had adverse reactions to the drug.

☺ The study found that 17% of the patients had adverse reactions to the drug.

~ (Tilde)

13.70 | The tilde, a symbol that dates back more than 3,000 years, is commonly used as a diacritical mark over certain letters to indicate various sounds in Spanish, Portuguese, and some Baltic languages.

13.71 | When the tilde is used in a manner that modifies a value, as in *~ 100 miles*, it is the equivalent of "approximately." Thus, *~ 100 miles* means approximately 100 miles. The tilde also can denote "similar to" or "of the same magnitude," so *x* ~ *y* means *x* is similar to *y*.

13.72 | In dictionaries, the tilde may be used as a substitute for the current word being defined.

> Wherever (adv.) anywhere at all; " ~ he goes, she will follow."

13.73 | The tilde is sometimes called a "swung dash" or "approximation sign." The symbol used for this purpose in typography is wider than the standard tilde; however, the ASCII character available in word processors commonly doubles for both.

13.74 | The tilde appears in some website URLs, and it usually points to a user's home directory. For instance, some universities provide students with free email and server space for a personal website, and the URL pointing to that website may contain a tilde.

> https://www.cs.tut.fi/~jkorpela/tilde.htm

The above is the Web address of a page that resides on a server at Tempere University of Technology in Finland. The site owner's username is *jkorpela*; the tilde is part of the URL that points to that user's homepage. As an amusing aside, at the time of this writing, the content displayed at this Web url is an essay entitled, *Why Tilde (~) Should Not Be Used in Web Addresses (URLs)*.

/ (Slash, Solidus, Stroke, or Virgule)

13.80 | The slash is a forward slanting line that dates back to the Middle Ages. Originally, it was used as a comma, and two forward slashes (//) represented a dash. Today, the symbol is extensively used in math and technology. It is a standard character in filenames and paths on computer drives, and at the least, two slashes appear in every Web address, placed together after the obligatory *http:* or *https:* prefix. When the symbol is used in computer-related contexts, it is usually called a "forward slash."

> Please delete the file "/users/home/mystuff/dumbgossip.txt" from your laptop drive.

> You can browse the Spectrum Ink homepage at
> http://vu.org/books/

The forward slash is sometimes confused with the backslash (written as one word) in file names and paths. The confusion arises from the fact that the backslash is used as a file path component separator on Windows computers; the forward slash serves the same purpose on UNIX-based operating systems.

13.81 | The forward slash can specify command-line options on some computer operating systems (DOS, Windows, OS/2). On a Windows machine, typing *dir /s* will display files in a specified directory and all subdirectories; typing *dir /p* will cause the directory display to pause after each full screen of information.

13.82 | The slash is sometimes used as a symbol that replaces the conjunction "or," such as you might find on a survey form: *Have you ever been arrested? Y/N.*

13.83 | The slash is used occasionally to define travel routes.

> London/Paris/Munich are destinations on the summer tour.

13.84 | The slash is commonly used in math, where it is called the "fraction slash" and separates the elements of a standard fraction, as in *1/2, 1/16*, and the like.

13.85 | In math and computer programming, the slash is often used as a division symbol. The equation *12 ÷ 2 = 6* can be expressed as *12/2 = 6* or *12 / 2 = 6.* Both forms, with and without a space before and after the slash, are acceptable in most style guides.

13.86 | In some programming languages, non-executable comments are set off by a slash paired with an asterisk, placed on the left side of the comment, and paired inversely on the right. Similarly, two slashes placed before a comment may be used for the same purpose. Inserting comments into program code allows the programmer to explain what specific lines of code are supposed to do, and setting off the comments in this manner makes them non-executable.

```
/* This is a comment */

// This is also a comment

/*
This is a multi-line comment.
Notice how the opening and closing
slash-asterisk pairings are used.
*/
```

Protocols for inserting comments into executable code vary from one programming language to another. When a comment block is written correctly, it won't execute when the program runs. If it is written incorrectly, running the code will probably throw an error and cause the program to crash. In this case, the program will not run until the error condition has been rectified.

13.87 | The slash is used as a calendar date separator. Thus, January 20, 2018 may be written as 1/20/2018 (or 20/1/2018 in some parts of the world). In America, the month typically is written first in a date, followed by the day and year. This contrasts with many other parts of the world—Europe, most of Asia, Australia, Central America, and South America—where the date is expressed as day/month/year.

_ (Underscore)

The underscore, also called the understrike, underline, or low line, is a throwback to manual typewriters. The symbol had its own dedicated key, and it was used to underline text for emphasis. First, you would type the text, then backspace as many times as necessary, and then repeatedly press the Underscore key to underline the text. It was common practice to underline titles of books, songs, films, and the like because typewriters did not offer an italics font for that purpose. Today, many word processing software applications streamline this task, and titles are generally italicized, but the underscore still is used in numerous ways.

13.90 | The underscore appears in some email addresses, website URLs, usernames on social media sites, and names of computer files. It serves no special purpose other than adding one more usable character to the standard set of letters and numbers.

>bill_smith@mydomain.com
>
>your_domain.com
>
>http://mydomain.com/some_file.html
>
>my_favorite_books.txt

13.91 | The underscore is still utilized in the present day to emphasize words and phrases in email messages and in online chat when the option to type bold or italicized text is not available to users. The asterisk is likewise used for this purpose.

>☺ Hey Alice, I have some _really_ exciting news!
>
>☺ Hey Alice, I have some *really* exciting news!

Some word processor programs will convert words and phrases typed within a pair of underscores to italics automatically. For example, if you type _important_ in Microsoft Word, the program will auto-convert it to *important*.

13.92 | Underscores are used in a number of ways in programming. One or more underscores can be used to link multi-word identifiers together in languages that do not support spaces in identifiers; for instance, *column_total*. This is an alternative to using camel case, in which the first letter of each word is capitalized, but no spaces or other characters are placed between the words, as *ColumnTotal*.

Some programming languages give special meaning to variables or other code prefixed with a single underscore, such as *_inputfield*, or even a double underscore, which in some languages (PHP) indicates an internal or otherwise special variable.

Conclusion

Thank you for reading this primer on English punctuation and capitalization. We hope you've enjoyed the book and that it will help you to improve your writing by providing a quick overview of essential punctuation rules, and a handy reference guide as you self-edit and proofread your manuscripts.

Please post a review! If you enjoyed this book, please take a minute to visit your favorite online bookseller and post a review. Even a brief review with just a sentence or two will be greatly appreciated and will help spread the word about this book to others. Thank you!

The author/editor of this book has published another writing handbook that delves deeper into English grammar and style. *Elements of Style 2017* includes many of the punctuation rules discussed here, but goes on to offer an in-depth roundup of grammar and style rules for writers, students, and others who must edit or proofread books, term papers, and other documents. The grammar rules in *Elements of Style 2017* are fully up-to-date and will guide you through the creative process of writing, revising, self-editing, and proofreading from start to finish, helping you produce grammar-perfect writing every time.

Browse the publisher's website at http://vu.org/books/elements for details, or pick up a copy of the e-book and paperback editions on Amazon.com at http://amzn.to/2iORqTV

Glossary

Punctuation marks

Colon :

Comma ,

Dash -

Ellipsis ... or . . .

En dash –

Em dash —

Exclamation point !

Parentheses ( )

Semicolon ;

Symbols

Ampersand &

Asterisk *

At sign @

Degree sign °

Ditto mark "

Cent sign ¢

Dollar sign $

Hash, pound, or number sign #

Percent sign %

Tilde ~

Slash, solidus, or virgule /

Underscore _

Vocabulary

Adjective: word, phrase, or clause that describes a noun or a pronoun

Adverb: word, phrase, or clause that modifies the meaning of a verb, an adjective, or another adverb

Antecedent: noun or noun phrase referenced by a pronoun

Appositive: noun or noun phrase that identifies, describes, or modifies the noun or pronoun placed immediately before it

Article: an adjective that specifically refers to another word; the three articles are: *the, a,* and *an*

Collective noun: a noun that refers to a group, as *family, staff, crew*

Complete sentence: a complete thought with a subject and a verb

Compound predicate: a sentence with one subject and two verbs

Compound sentence: a sentence with more than one subject or predicate, typically joined by a conjunction such as *and, but, or*

Conditional clause: expresses a condition using a word such as *if, when, though*

Conjunction: a word that connects clauses, such as *and, but, or*

Conjunctive adverb: an adverb that connects two independent clauses, such as *however, moreover, nevertheless, therefore, thus, indeed*

Connective: word or phrase that links clauses or sentences; typically, a conjunction, such as *and, but, or*

Coordinate adjectives: descriptive words that can be used in any order without changing the meaning of the sentence

Dangling modifier: a word or phrase, often at the start of a sentence, written in such a way that it modifies the wrong word or phrase, or it modifies nothing

Dependent clause: phrase with a subject and verb, but not a complete sentence

Exclamatory: word or phrase that expresses surprise, anger or shock

First person: in writing, a point of view or "voice" that refers to the speaker or a group that includes the speaker (*I, we*)

Full stop: punctuation mark; a period

Gerund: a verb form ending in *-ing* used as a noun

Indirect question: a question within a sentence that is not stated directly; a question in reported speech

Indirect quotation: paraphrase of someone else's words.

Infinitive: a verb form, often beginning with *to*, that lacks an inflection binding it to a subject or tense, as *to run, to write*

Interjection: word or short phrase expressing a sudden reaction or emotion, as *Oh!, Ouch!, Wow!*

Interrogative statement: a declarative sentence with the structure of a question that states a fact rather than asks a question

Interrogatory: a question

Main clause: the principle part of a sentence that can stand alone

Modifier: a word, phrase, or clause that modifies, describes, or restricts the meaning of another word or phrase

Nonrestrictive modifier: phrase or clause that adds descriptive detail but is not essential; if omitted from the sentence, the meaning does not change.

Noun: word that names a person, place, thing, quality, idea, action, state of existence, etc.

Object: word or phrase, typically a noun or pronoun, that receives or is affected by the action of a verb

Ordinal number: a number that defines an item's rank in a series, such as *first, second, third.*

Parenthetical expression: a nonrestrictive or nonessential phrase; a word or phrase inserted into a sentence that can be removed without changing the meaning of the sentence.

Participial phrase: phrase that begins with a present or a past participle

Participle: a verb form ending in *-ed* or *-ing* and used as an adjective or a noun

Past participle: verb form ending in *-ed*

Phrase: an incomplete sentence; a group of two or more words that lack a subject and verb required to form a clause

Phrases in apposition: two phrases, placed side by side, where one identifies the other in some different way.

Possessive case: a noun, pronoun, or adjective that shows ownership or possession, usually formed by adding an apostrophe and the letter *s* to the end of the word, as *Bob's* car, *Maria's* house

Predicate: element of a sentence that contains a verb and says something about the subject

Preposition: word that links a noun, pronoun, or phrase to other words in a sentence

Present participle: verb form ending in *-ing*

Principal clause: group of words that has a subject and predicate but does not form a complete sentence

Pronoun: a word that takes the place of a noun, such as *he, she, I, you, me, many, who, somebody, everybody*

Restrictive modifier: a word, phrase, or clause that modifies another element in a way that is essential to the main idea

Restrictive relative clause: phrase that gives essential information about the noun to which it refers

Run-on sentence: a sentence comprised of two full sentences run together with a conjunction or punctuation between them; also called a *fused sentence*

Second person: in writing, a point of view or "voice" that refers to the speaker's audience (*you*)

Sentence: group of words that expresses a complete thought or idea

Serial comma: the comma that sets off the final item in a list and precedes a connecting conjunction, such as *and, but, or* (also called an Oxford comma)

Tense: past, present, or future quality that expresses when the action of a verb happened, is happening, or will happen

Third person: point of view or "voice" that refers to someone other than the speaker or the speaker's audience (*he, she, it, they*)

Terminating mark: punctuation mark that ends a sentence, most often a full stop, but may also be a question mark, exclamation point, dash (where a sentence is abruptly interrupted), or ellipsis (sentence trails off)

Verb: a word that describes, an occurrence, or a state of being

More Books from Spectrum Ink

Elements of Style 2017
Compiled and Edited by Richard De A'Morelli

(Nonfiction Reference/Writing)

Elements of Style 2017 provides a convenient, all-in-one reference to grammar, style, and punctuation rules. Clear, concise writing is essential in today's world. For an author, a well-edited manuscript may bring an acceptance letter from a publisher or agent; or if you self-publish, it could generate positive reviews and sales. For students, an impressed instructor could mean an A grade; and on the job, a well-written report could mean a pay raise, a promotion, or the success of a business venture.

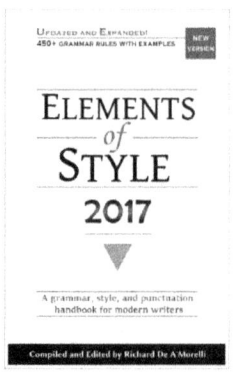

Learn how to improve your grammar and style, and polish your writing to perfection with *Elements of Style 2017*.

Available online or visit: http://vu.org/books/elements

ISBN Numbers	Editions
978-1-988236-26-1	MOBI/Kindle
978-1-988236-27-8	EPUB Digital
978-1-988236-28-5	Paperback
978-1-088236-31-5	Paperback Large Print

Live Well. Be Happy.
by Richard De A'Morelli

(Inspirational/Self-Help)

This book is about your life and your search for happiness. It will help you to realize that you can change your life by changing how you think and react to the world around you. You will learn steps you can take to stay sane, positive, and balanced in a crazy world. And you will discover how making simple changes in your daily routine can help you find your path to happiness.

In these pages, you will learn that happiness in life depends on the choices you make, staying positive, and never giving up on your hopes and dreams. You'll discover simple methods to reduce stress, overcome depression, build confidence, and conquer unhealthy habits. You will also learn how to stay balanced and maintain your peace of mind using natural techniques such as deep relaxation, visualization, rhythm breathing, and meditation.

This inspiring little book reminds us that life is short, and we must make the most of the precious time we are given. If you have been looking for a book that will encourage you to change your life and give you a helping hand to move forward, this short course in modern living may be that inspiration. The book also makes a wonderful gift for someone in need of encouragement and a step-by-step approach to getting their life on a positive track.

Buy online or visit: http://vu.org/books/live-well/live-well

978-1-988234-09-3	MOBI/Kindle
978-1-988234-08-6	EPUB Digital
978-1-988234-04-8	Paperback
978-1-988236-46-9	Paperback (retail)
978-1-988236-47-6	Hardcover

As A Man Thinks

Edited by Richard De A'Morelli

(Inspirational/Self-Help)

This special edition of James Allen's classic book *As a Man Thinketh* explores how the power of thought affects you on every level, and how you can take control of your life and destiny. The way you think creates every condition in your life, good and bad. If you have been beset by disappointment and failure, the empowering wisdom in this book can change your life. You will learn how to use the power of your mind to build confidence, unlock hidden talents, cope with depression and stress, overcome habits, and achieve health and vitality. Learn how to use these timeless insights to build a bright future and become the master of your destiny.

This edition retains the flavor of James Allen's practical advice but has been updated to a modern style that is easy to follow and enjoyable to read. Also, the book has been expanded—each chapter includes additional insights, explanations, and points to remember that can empower you to change your life by changing the way you think.

Buy online or visit: http://vu.org/books/as-a-man-thinks

ISBN Numbers	Editions
978-1-988236-08-7	MOBI/Kindle
978-1-988236-09-4	EPUB Digital
978-1-988236-10-0	Paperback
978-1-988236-11-7	Paperback Large Print
978-1-988236-12-4	Hardcover Edition

Apocalypse Orphan

By Tim Allen

(Science Fiction-Fantasy)

Commander Orlando Iron Wolf is aboard the International Space Station when a blinking light on his computer console alerts him to a fast moving comet headed for a collision with planet Earth.

With no way to stop the impending doomsday, the world descends into panic and anarchy. Massive transport ships are built to colonize the moon, and evacuation of a chosen few begins.

After a shuttle mission to study the approaching comet goes awry, Wolf is forced into cryogenic deep sleep, and the onboard computer assumes control of the ship.

Wolf awakens 50,000 years later to a wildly different earth. Endowed with incredible strength, he finds himself caught in a war between primitive tribes, and his survival depends on Syn, an advanced computer intelligence who has fallen in love with him.

Will Wolf be able to help restore Earth to its past glory or is civilization doomed to fail?

Available online or visit: http://vu.org/books/ao

ISBN Numbers	Editions
978-1-988236-00-1	MOBI/Kindle
978-1-988236-07-0	EPUB Digital
978-1-988236-01-8	Paperback
978-1-088236-02-5	Paperback Large Print
978-1-988236-03-2	Hardcover Edition

Notes

Notes

Notes

Notes

Notes

Notes